D0122131

THE THIRD DAY

THE THIRD DAY

Hank Hanegraaff

Foreword by Lee Strobel

W PUBLISHING GROUP™

www.wpublishinggroup.com

A Division of Thomas Nelson, Inc.
www.ThomasNelson.com

To Everett Jacobson,
"a friend who sticks closer than a brother."
—PROVERBS 18:24

THE THIRD DAY

by Hank Hanegraaff

Copyright © 2003 by Hank Hanegraaff.
Published by W Publishing Group, a unit of Thomas Nelson, Inc.,
P. O. Box 141000, Nashville, Tennessee 37214.

Text excerpted and revised from *Resurrection* by Hank Hanegraaff
(Nashville: W Publishing Group, 2000).

Unless otherwise indicated, Scripture quotations used in this book are
from *The Holy Bible, New International Version,* copyright © 1973, 1978,
1984, International Bible Society. Used by permission of
Zondervan Bible Publishers.

Scriptures noted NASB are taken from the *New American Standard Bible,*
copyright © 1960, 1962, 1963, 1968, 1971, 1972, 1973, 1975, 1977
by the Lockman Foundation. All rights reserved. Used by permission.

ISBN 0-8499-1755-7

Printed in the United States of America
03 04 05 06 07 PHX 9 8 7 6 5 4 3 2 1

CONTENTS

fOREWORD

As a journalist at the *Chicago Tribune,* I saw plenty of dead bodies—victims of fires, crimes, auto accidents, street gang wars, and crime syndicate retribution. But I had never seen anyone come back to life. That was the stuff of fantasies, mythology, and legend. After all, we live in a scientific age. Believing in the idea of someone being resurrected from the dead was simply no longer tenable.

At least, that's what I thought until I checked out the facts for myself. Using my journalism experience and legal training, I investigated the most audacious claim of history: that Jesus of Nazareth returned from the dead and thus authenticated his claim to being the unique Son of God.

I thought it would take only a short time to dismiss that story as a hoax, a myth, or a misunderstanding. Instead, the more I delved into the historical evidence, the more convinced I became that Jesus did return to life on the third day. There was, in the words of Sir Lionel Luckhoo, the world's most successful lawyer, "absolutely no room for doubt." Based on the evidence I abandoned atheism and embraced Jesus as my forgiver, leader, and friend.

My investigation into the historical truth of the Resurrection would have been considerably easier if Hank Hanegraaff's concise and compelling book *The Third Day* had been available to me back then. With laser-beam focus, Hank zeroes in on the most convincing facts that back up Jesus' death, his empty tomb, his postresurrection appearances, and the subsequent transformation of those who encountered him.

Hank's treatment is succinct but not superficial. He marshals the evidence with the force of a prosecutor, shedding the peripheral and highlighting the important. What's more, he answers the "so what" question by demonstrating the relevance of the Resurrection to every individual—and even to the cosmos itself.

I remember asking Resurrection expert Gary Habermas why he has spent a lifetime unearthing evidence to document Jesus' return from the dead. "It's very simple," he replied. "You see, every single shred of evidence for the resurrection of Jesus Christ is also evidence for *my* eventual resurrection."

That's why the evidence in this book should be important to you, too. Read *The Third Day* to boost your faith, to arm you with answers for your skeptical friends, to prompt your worship of the Son of God. And read it because all the evidence for the resurrection of Jesus is also proof that you, too, will conquer the grave if you follow him.

"I am the resurrection and the life," Jesus said in John 11:25. "He who believes in me will live, even though he dies."

—LEE STROBEL
Author, *The Case for Christ* and
The Case for Faith

ACKNOWLEDGMENTS

FIRST, I WOULD LIKE TO ACKNOWLEDGE the board and staff of the Christian Research Institute for their encouragement. Furthermore, I would like to express appreciation to the staff of W Publishing Group for their support. Finally, I would like to acknowledge Kathy and the kids—Michelle, Katie, David, John, Mark, Hank Jr., Christina, Paul Stephen, Faith, and baby Grace—who have blessed me beyond measure! Above all, I am supremely thankful to the Lord Jesus Christ—because he lives we can face the future without fear.

Introduction

Before you start down the road to resurrection—a pilgrimage that for some will be measured in days and for others in decades—allow me to start by underscoring the importance of the trek. This is not just any journey; it is a journey of enormous consequence. You see, without resurrection there is no hope. Indeed, without resurrection, there is no Christianity.

As you travel through these pages, you will encounter attacks on resurrection ranging from Judaism, which swears it never happened; to Jehovah's Witnesses, who suggest that Jesus' physical body was discarded, destroyed, or dissolved into gasses; and to Jesus Seminar fellows who say that resurrection is wishful thinking.

When you reach your destination, however, you will

have encountered all the evidence necessary to demonstrate not only that Christ's resurrection is an immutable fact of history, but that your own resurrection is just as certain.

We begin the journey with chapter 1, titled "Mythologies." In this chapter, we travel through a never-ending stream of imaginative stories designed to demonstrate that the Resurrection is a crutch for weak-minded Christians. In the following four chapters, I demonstrate in memorable fashion that far from being a gargantuan fraud, the resurrection of Jesus Christ is the greatest *feat* in the annals of recorded history.

In the final two chapters, we discover that resurrection is a reality for everyone reading these words. As has been well said, the death rate is one per person, and everyone alive is going to make it. Some will be physically resurrected to eternity with the Savior in a new heaven and new earth, others to eternal separation from the Savior.[1] I urge you to read on and realize that resurrection is not merely an important issue; an understanding of the biblical nature of the resurrection will literally transform the way you live your life today.

ONE

Mythologies

When they had crucified him, above his head they placed the written charge against him: THIS IS JESUS, THE KING OF THE JEWS. Those who passed by hurled insults at him, shaking their heads and saying, "You who are going to destroy the temple and build it in three days, save yourself! Come down from the cross, if you are the Son of God!"

In the same way the chief priests, the teachers of the law, and the elders mocked him—and the robbers who were crucified with him also heaped insults on him.

About the ninth hour, Jesus cried out in a loud voice, "Eloi, Eloi, lama sabachthani?"—which means, "My God, My God, why have you forsaken me?"

Then Jesus, knowing that the Passover plot was nearing completion, cried out, "I am thirsty."

As if on cue, an unidentified friend of Joseph of Arimathea ran, filled a sponge with a sleeping potion, put it on a stick, and offered it to Jesus to drink.

When he had received it, Jesus cried out, "It is finished." With that, he bowed his head and swooned.

Because the Jews did not want the bodies left on the crosses during the Sabbath, they asked Pilate to have the legs broken and the bodies taken down. But when they came to Jesus and found that he was already dead, they did not break his legs. Instead, one of the soldiers pierced Jesus' side with a spear.

As evening approached, Joseph of Arimathea went boldly to Pilate and asked for the body of Jesus. He took the body, wrapped it in a clean linen cloth, and placed it in a tomb cut out of rock.

There Joseph and the unidentified Jew worked feverishly to nurse Jesus back to life.

Tragically, the Roman spear led to the death of Christ and the virtual destruction of the Passover plot. Jesus regained consciousness only long enough to cry out, "Do not let me die in vain. Deceive my disciples into believing I have overcome death and the grave." With that, he bowed his head and died. Immediately Joseph and the unidentified Jew took the body of Jesus and disposed of it.

During the next forty days the unidentified Jew appeared to the disciples and through many convincing fabrications deluded them into believing that he was the resurrected Christ. Beginning with Moses and all the Prophets, he explained to them everything that the Scriptures had taught concerning the Messiah—how he should suffer, die, and be raised again. The hearts of the disciples burned within as they believed the lie. To this very day, the Passover plot engi-

neered by Jesus, Joseph, and the unidentified Jew continues to delude millions into believing that Jesus Christ has risen from the dead.

—Mythologies 27:35–50*

In 1965, Hugh Schonfield published a 287-page volume titled *The Passover Plot*.[1] In this runaway bestseller, Schonfield contends that Jesus "deliberately plotted" his crucifixion and subsequent resurrection. According to *The Passover Plot*, "Jesus contrived to be arrested the night before the Passover, fully aware that he would be nailed to the cross the following day, but taken down before the onset of the Sabbath in accordance with Jewish law. He would survive the agony of but three hours on the cross."[2] Rather than suffering fatal torment, Jesus merely swooned.

To ensure Jesus' safe removal from the cross, Joseph and an unidentified Jew concocted a plan in which Jesus would be given "not the traditional vinegar but a drug that would render him unconscious and make him appear dead. He would then be cut down from the cross in a deathlike trance, removed by accomplices to the tomb where he would be nursed back to

---

*Adapted from the Gospel of Matthew (NIV) but radically altered to accommodate Hugh Schonfield's "Passover plot" hypothesis

health and then 'resurrected.'"[3] Thus, the tomb was empty due not to resurrection, but to resuscitation.

This new interpretation of the life and death of Jesus captured the imagination of the world. Magazines and ministers immediately lauded it as perhaps the most important book published in a decade. *Time* magazine contended, "Schonfield . . . does not discredit Christ. Instead, he argues that Christ was indeed the Messiah—the Son of Man, as he thought of himself, but not the Son of God—who had been foretold by Jewish prophets of old, and that this is glory enough."[4] Bible scholar William Barclay called *The Passover Plot* "a book of enormous learning and erudition, meticulously documented."[5] This despite the fact that Schonfield himself admitted that it is "an imaginative reconstruction of the personality, aims and activities of Jesus," in which such characters as the unidentified Jew emerge out of thin air.[6]

THE SWOON HYPOTHESIS

While the critics of historic Christianity have passionately proclaimed the virtues of Schonfield and his scholarship, *The Passover Plot* is little more than a novel regurgitation of swoon hypotheses that were popular in the first half of the nineteenth century. As noted investigative journalist Lee Strobel points out in *The Case for Christ,* the swoon hypothesis is an urban legend that is continually being resuscitated.[7]

Despite the fact that the swoon hypothesis has been soundly refuted by academia,[8] it is still regurgitated ad nauseum in the public arena. Swoon theorists dismiss the Resurrection by contending that Jesus never really died on the cross; instead, he merely fainted and was later revived. A never-ending stream of imaginative stories has flowed from this basic hypothesis.

In 1929, D. H. Lawrence fantasized that, after surviving crucifixion, Jesus ended up in Egypt. There he fell in love with the priestess Isis.[9] In 1972, Donovan Joyce published *The Jesus Scroll.*[10] Christian philosopher Gary Habermas explains that, in Joyce's rendition of the story, Jesus was apparently revived by a doctor who had been planted in the tomb ahead of time. The doctor was assisted by none other than Jesus' uncle, Joseph of Arimathea. In Joyce's fanciful reconstruction, Jesus is an "eighty-year-old defender of Masada who apparently died while fighting the Romans during the Jewish revolt of A.D. 66–73." In this scrolled autobiography, Jesus is married to Mary Magdalene, is a revolutionary zealot who wars with the Romans, and in the end retires as a monk at Qumran.[11]

In 1992, Barbara Thiering produced an even more outrageous version of the swoon hypothesis.[12] Historian Edwin Yamauchi points out that Thiering, who is a professor at the University of Sydney in Australia, uses the New Testament as a "coded commentary" to reinterpret the Dead Sea Scrolls. In Thiering's mind-boggling tale, Jesus is crucified along with Simon Magus and Judas at Qumran, imbibes snake poison to fake his death, upon recovering marries Mary Magdalene, and later falls in love with Lydia of Philippi. Despite the fact that Thiering's revolting reconstruction is devoid of rhyme or reason, it has received rave reviews in a wide variety of public forums, ranging from radio to television.[13]

THE TWIN HYPOTHESIS

The swoon hypothesis is not the only novel notion that critics of Christianity have used to explain away the Resurrection. Another is the twin hypothesis.[14] In a 1995 debate with Christian apologist William Lane Craig, philosopher Robert Greg Cavin contended that Jesus had an identical twin brother, whom he names Hurome.[15] Hurome is separated from Jesus at birth and does not see him again until the time of the Crucifixion. Upon stumbling into Jerusalem, he sees his mirror image on the cross and realizes that the Jesus of Nazareth he had previously heard so much about was in reality his identical twin. He immediately concocts a messianic mission for Christ and carries it out by stealing the body and pretending to be the resurrected Christ.[16] During the debate, Craig summarizes Cavin's version of the story as follows:

> Jesus had an unknown identical twin who impersonated Jesus after the crucifixion, thereby convincing people that he was risen from the dead. Remember the movie *Dave*—you know the one where the presidential double takes over the U.S. presidency when the real president falls into a coma—well [Cavin's] theory is a sort of Dave theory of the Resurrection. Jesus' unknown twin stole Jesus' body out of the tomb and impersonated Jesus before the disciples. Now, if you are wondering why nobody knew about Jesus' twin brother that's because on [Cavin's] theory unbeknownst to Mary and Joseph their real baby got accidentally switched with one member of a pair of identical twins. So the person that we call Jesus wasn't really Mary's child at all and his twin brother grew up independently of him.

Craig goes on to say that theories like the twin hypothesis may make great comedy, but no one should take them seriously—particularly theories like that of Cavin, whose research has forced him to agree that Christ was fatally tormented, that the tomb was empty, that the disciples were convinced Jesus had appeared to them, and that as a result of the Resurrection their lives were utterly transformed.

THE MUSLIM HYPOTHESIS

Other hypotheses used to explain away the biblical account of the Resurrection emanate from world religions, such as Islam. From a Muslim perspective, Jesus was never crucified and thus never resurrected.[17] As Christian philosopher Norman Geisler explains, orthodox Muslims have traditionally held that "Jesus was not crucified on the cross, but that God made someone else look like Jesus and this person was mistakenly crucified as Christ. And the words 'God raised him up unto Himself' have often been taken to mean that Jesus was taken up alive to heaven without dying."[18]

There are a wide variety of opinions in the Muslim world as to whom God substituted for Jesus. Possible candidates range from Judas Iscariot to Pilate to Simon of Cyrene or even to one of Christ's inner circle. Some Muslims contend that one of the disciples volunteered to take on the likeness of Christ, while other Muslims contend that God involuntarily caused one of Christ's enemies to take on his appearance. Geisler goes on to note that "the view that Judas replaced Christ on the cross was again recently popularized in the Muslim world by *The Gospel of Barnabas.*"[19]

Muslims also disagree on what happened to Jesus. A majority, however, "contend that Jesus escaped the cross by being taken up to heaven and that one day he will come back to earth and play a central role in the future events. Based on some of the alleged sayings of Muhammad, Muslims believe that, just before the end of time, Jesus will come back to earth, kill the Antichrist (al-Dajjal), kill all pigs, break the cross, destroy the synagogues and churches, establish the religion of Islam, live for forty years, and then he will be buried in the city of Medina beside the prophet Muhammad."[20]

THE WATCHTOWER HYPOTHESIS

Other theories concerning the resurrection of Jesus Christ can be found in the kingdom of the cults. Jehovah's Witnesses, for example, are not only famous for denying the deity of

Jesus Christ, but for denying his bodily resurrection as well.[21] Their contention is that Jesus was created by God as the archangel Michael,[22] that during his earthly sojourn he became merely human, and that after his crucifixion he was re-created as an immaterial spirit creature. As the Watchtower organization puts it, "the King Christ Jesus was put to death in the flesh and was resurrected an invisible spirit creature. Therefore the world will see him no more. He went to prepare a heavenly place for his associate heirs, 'Christ's body,' for they too will be invisible spirit creatures."[23]

Furthermore, Jehovah's Witnesses assert that a physical resurrection would not have been a tremendous triumph; it would have been a hopeless humiliation. In their view, it would mean that after reigning as the archangel Michael, Jesus was reduced to a human being and did not subsequently regain his former status as an exalted spirit creature. Thus, according to the Watchtower Bible and Tract Society, "Jesus did not take his human body to heaven to be forever a man in heaven. Had he done so, that would have left him even lower than the angels. . . . God did not purpose for Jesus to be humiliated thus forever by being a fleshly man forever. No, but after he had sacrificed his perfect manhood, God raised him to deathless life as a glorious spirit creature."[24]

To explain away the empty tomb, Jehovah's Witnesses argue that the physical body of Jesus was discarded and destroyed. In the words of the Watchtower, "The human body of flesh, which Jesus Christ laid down forever as a ransom sacrifice, was disposed of by God's power."[25] Thus, instead of rising from the dead, "the fleshly body of Jesus Christ was disposed of on earth by Almighty God and not taken to heaven by Jesus."[26] In the view of Watchtower founder Charles Taze Russell, the body that hung on the cross either "dissolved into gasses" or is "preserved somewhere as the grand memorial of God's love."[27]

Finally, it should be noted that Jehovah's Witnesses attempt to explain away the postresurrection appearances of Christ by suggesting that "the bodies in which Jesus manifested himself to his disciples after his return to life were not the body in which he was nailed to the tree. They were merely materialized for the occasion, resembling on one or two occasions the body in which he died, but on the majority of occasions being unrecognizable by his most intimate disciples."[28] If Jehovah's Witnesses are correct, Jesus fooled his disciples into thinking he had physically risen from the grave by appearing in a variety of disparate bodies. In their words, "he appeared in different bodies. He appeared and disappeared just as the angels had done, because he was resurrected as a spirit creature. Only because Thomas would not believe did Jesus appear in a body like that in which he had died."[29]

GREATEST FEAT OR GARGANTUAN FRAUD?

If devotees of the kingdom of the cults, adherents of world religions, or liberal scholars are correct, the biblical account of the Resurrection is fiction, fantasy, or a gargantuan fraud. If, on the other hand, Christianity is factually reliable, the Resurrection is the greatest feat in human history. As Christian apologist Josh McDowell puts it, "After more than seven hundred hours of studying this subject and thoroughly investigating its foundation, I have come to the conclusion that the resurrection of Jesus Christ is one of the most wicked, vicious, heartless hoaxes ever foisted upon the minds of men, OR it is the most fantastic fact of history."[30]

Wilbur Smith points out that, from the very first, the Christian church has unanimously borne witness to the immutable fact of Christ's resurrection. Says Smith, "It is what we may call one of the great fundamental doctrines and convictions of the church, and so penetrates the literature of the New Testament, that if you lifted out every passage in which a reference is made to the Resurrection, you would have a collection of writings so mutilated that what remained could not be understood."[31]

The book of Acts is a classic case in point. In Acts 1, Matthias is chosen to replace Judas as a witness of the Resurrection. In Acts 2, Peter, in his powerful Pentecost proclamation, thunders, "Brothers, I can tell you confidently that the patriarch David died and was buried, and his tomb is here to this day. But he was a prophet and knew that God had promised him on oath that he would place one of his descendants on his throne. Seeing what was ahead, he spoke of the resurrection of the Christ, that he was not abandoned to the grave, nor did his body see decay. God has raised this Jesus to life, and we are all witnesses of the fact" (vv. 29–32).

In Acts 3, at a place called Solomon's Colonnade, Peter said to the men of Israel, "The God of Abraham, Isaac and Jacob, the God of our fathers, has glorified his servant Jesus. You handed him over to be killed, and you disowned him before Pilate, though he had decided to let him go. You disowned the Holy and Righteous One and asked that a murderer be released to you. You killed the author of life, but God raised him from the dead. We are witnesses of this" (vv. 13–15). In Acts 4, we read that the priests, the captain of the temple guard, and the Sadducees were so disturbed by the preaching of Peter and John that they threw them into prison for "proclaiming in Jesus the resurrection of the dead" (v. 2). Likewise, in Acts 5, the apostles face a flogging for testifying that God "raised Jesus from the dead" (v. 30).

In Acts 10, Peter, at a large gathering of people in the house of Cornelius, testifies to the Resurrection, saying, "We are witnesses of everything [Jesus] did in the country of the Jews and in Jerusalem. They killed him by hanging him on a tree, but God raised him from the dead on the third day and caused him to be seen. He was not seen by all the people, but by witnesses whom God had already chosen—by us who ate and drank with him after he rose from the dead" (vv. 39–41).

In Acts 13, the spotlight moves from Peter to Paul. After leaving Perga, Paul went on to Pisidian, Antioch. There in his synagogue sermon this persecutor-turned-proselytizer proclaims that the people of Jerusalem and their rulers asked Pilate to have Jesus condemned to death despite the fact that they found no warrant for his crucifixion. Says Paul:

"When they had carried out all that was written about him, they took him down from the tree and laid him in a tomb. But God raised him from the dead, and for many days he was seen by those who had traveled with him from Galilee to Jerusalem. They are now his witnesses to our people.

"We tell you the good news: What God promised our fathers he has fulfilled for us, their children, by raising up Jesus. As it is written in the second Psalm: 'You are my Son; today I have become your Father.' The fact that God raised him from the dead, never to decay, is stated in these words: 'I will give you the holy and sure blessings promised to David." So it is stated elsewhere: "You will not let your Holy One see decay.'

For when David had served God's purpose in his own generation, he fell asleep; he was buried with his fathers and his body decayed. But the one whom God raised from the dead did not see decay." (Acts 13:29–37)

In Acts 17, we find Paul in Athens, passionately preaching the good news about Jesus and the Resurrection. After a group of Epicurean and Stoic philosophers brought him to a meeting of the Areopagus, Paul stood up and addressed the crowd as follows:

"Men of Athens! I see that in every way you are very religious. For as I walked around and looked carefully at your objects of worship, I even found an altar with this inscription: TO AN UNKNOWN GOD. Now what you worship as something unknown I am going to proclaim to you.

"The God who made the world and everything in it is the Lord of heaven and earth and does not live in temples built by hands. And he is not served by human hands, as if he needed anything, because he himself gives all men life and breath and everything else. From one man he made every nation of men, that they should inhabit the whole earth; and he determined the times set for them and the exact places where they should live. God did this so that men would seek him and perhaps reach out for him and find him, though he is not far from each one of us. 'For in him we live and move and have our being.' As some of your own poets have said, 'We are his offspring.'

"Therefore since we are God's offspring, we should not think that the divine being is like gold or silver or stone—an image made by man's design and skill. In the past God overlooked such ignorance, but now he commands all people everywhere to repent. For he has set a day when he will judge the world with justice by the man he has appointed. He has given proof of this to all men by raising him from the dead."

When they heard about the resurrection of the dead, some of them sneered, but others said, "We want to hear you again on this subject." (Acts 17:22–32)

Many other such passages from Dr. Luke's Acts of the Apostles could be cited. Suffice it to say, Wilbur Smith was absolutely right. Without the Resurrection, not only Acts, but the whole of Scripture would be a disfigured document devoid of definition. The Resurrection so radically changed the lives of Christ's followers that it was engraved on their tombs and depicted on the walls of their catacombs. In addition, "it entered deeply into Christian hymnology; it became one of the most vital themes of the great apologetic writings of the first four centuries; it was the theme constantly dwelt upon in the preaching of the ante-Nicene and post-Nicene period. It entered at once into the creedal formulae of the church; it is in our Apostles' Creed; it is in all the great creeds that followed."[32]

Smith goes on to note that "the burden of the good news or gospel was not 'Follow this Teacher and do your best,' but, 'Jesus and the Resurrection.' You cannot take that away from Christianity without radically altering its character and destroying its very identity."[33] Paul, along with the rest of the apostles, made it crystal-clear that no middle ground exists. The Resurrection is history or hoax, miracle or myth, fact or fantasy. Says Paul:

> If Christ has not been raised, our preaching is useless and so is your faith. More than that, we are then found to be false witnesses about God, for we have testified about God that he raised Christ from the dead. But he did not raise him if in fact the dead are not raised. For if the dead are not raised, then Christ has not been raised either. And if Christ has not been raised, your faith is futile; you are still in your sins. Then those also who have fallen asleep in Christ are lost. If only for this life we have hope in Christ, we are to be pitied more than all men. (1 Corinthians 15:14–19)

Preevangelism / Postevangelism

It is precisely because of the strategic importance of the Resurrection that each Christian must be prepared to defend its historicity. Thus, apologetics—the defense of the faith—has a dual purpose. On the one hand, apologetics involves preevangelism. In post-Christian America, few people are aware that belief in the Resurrection is not a blind leap into the dark, but faith founded on fact. It is historic and evidential. Thus, it is defensible. On the other hand, apologetics involves postevangelism. During an age in which the Resurrection is under siege, knowing how to defend its reliability serves to strengthen our faith.

The Resurrection is not merely important to the historic Christian faith; without it, there would be no Christianity. It is the singular doctrine that elevates Christianity above all other world religions. Through the Resurrection, Christ demonstrated that he does not stand in a line of peers with Abraham, Buddha, or Confucius. He is utterly unique. He has the power not only to lay down his life, but to take it up again.

Because of its centrality to Christianity, those who take the sacred name of Christ upon their lips must be prepared to defend the reliability of the Resurrection. To make the process memorable, I've developed the acronym FEAT. This acronym should serve as an enduring reminder that, far from being a gargantuan fraud, the Resurrection is the greatest feat in the annals of recorded history. As we will see in the following chapters, each letter in FEAT will serve to remind us of an undeniable fact of the Resurrection:

Fatal Torment

Empty Tomb

Appearances of Christ

Transformation

Two

Fatal Torment

From the sixth hour until the ninth hour darkness came over all the land. About the ninth hour Jesus cried out in a loud voice, "Eloi, Eloi, lama sabachthani?"—which means, "My God, my God, why have you forsaken me?"...And when Jesus had cried out again in a loud voice, he gave up his spirit. (Matthew 27: 45–46, 50)

THE FATAL SUFFERING OF JESUS CHRIST as recounted in the New Testament is one of the most well-established facts of ancient history. Even in today's modern age of scientific enlightenment, there is a virtual consensus among New Testament scholars, both conservative and liberal, that Jesus died on the cross, that he was buried in the tomb of Joseph of Arimathea, and that his death drove his disciples to despair.[1]

THE MEDICAL FACTS

The best medical minds of ancient and modern times have demonstrated beyond a shadow of a doubt that Christ's physical trauma was fatal.[2] His torment began in the Garden of Gethsemane after the emotional Last Supper. There Jesus experienced a medical condition known as hematidrosis. Tiny capillaries in his sweat glands ruptured, mixing sweat with blood. As a result, Christ's skin became extremely fragile.

The same night, Jesus was betrayed by Judas, disowned by Peter, and arrested by the temple guard. Before Caiaphas the high priest, he was mocked, beaten, and spat upon. The next morning, Jesus, battered, bruised, and bleeding, was led into the Praetorium. There Jesus was stripped and subjected to the brutality of Roman flogging. A whip replete with razor-sharp bones and lead balls reduced his body to quivering ribbons of bleeding flesh. As Christ slumped into the pool of his own blood, the soldiers threw a scarlet robe across his shoulders, thrust a scepter into his hand, and pressed sharp thorns into his scalp.

After they mocked him, they took the scepter out of his hand and repeatedly struck him on the head. Now Jesus was in critical condition. A heavy wooden beam was thrust upon Christ's bleeding body, and he was led away to a place called Golgotha. There the Lord experienced ultimate physical torture in the form of the cross. The Roman system of crucifixion had been fine-tuned to produce maximum pain. In fact, the word *excruciating* (literally "out of the cross") had to be invented to fully codify its horror.[3]

At "the place of the skull," the Roman soldiers drove thick, seven-inch iron spikes through Christ's hands[4] and feet. Waves of pain pulsated through Christ's body as the nails lacerated his nerves. Breathing became an agonizing endeavor as Christ pushed his tortured body upward to grasp small gulps of air. In the ensuing hours, he experienced cycles of joint-wrenching cramps, intermittent asphyxiation, and excruciating pain as his lacerated back moved up and down against the rough timber of the cross.

As the chill of death crept through his body, Jesus cried out, "*'Eloi, Eloi, lama sabachthani?'*—which means, 'My God, my God, why have you forsaken me?'" (Matthew 27:46). And in that anguished cry was encapsulated the greatest agony of all. For on the cross, Christ bore the sin and suffering of all humanity. And then with his passion complete, Jesus gave up his spirit.

Shortly thereafter, a Roman legionnaire drove his spear through the fifth interspace between the ribs, upward through the pericardium, and into Christ's heart. From the wound rushed forth blood and water, demonstrating conclusively that Jesus had suffered fatal torment.

In light of all the evidence, believing that Jesus merely swooned stretches credulity beyond the breaking point. It means that Christ survived several trials, a lack of sleep, the scourge, being spiked to a cross, and a spear wound in his side.

Adherence to some of the more implausible versions of the swoon hypothesis would take even more faith. It would entail believing that Jesus survived three days without medical attention, single-handedly rolled away an enormously heavy tombstone, subdued an armed guard, strolled around on pierced feet, and seduced his disciples into communicating the myth that he had conquered death while he lived out the remainder of his pathetic life in obscurity.

THE MEDICAL VERDICT

Dr. Alexander Metherell, a prominent physician who has thoroughly investigated the historical and medical facts regarding the death of Jesus Christ, drove a fatal stake through the heart of the swoon hypothesis. In an interview with investigative journalist Lee Strobel, Dr. Metherell pointed out that a person who had suffered the kind of excruciating torture recounted in the Gospels "would never have inspired his disciples to go out and proclaim that he's the Lord of life who had triumphed over the grave." Metherell went on to say that "after suffering that horrible abuse, with all the catastrophic blood loss and trauma, he would have looked so pitiful that his disciples would never have hailed him as a victorious conqueror of death; they would have felt sorry for him and tried to nurse him back to health." Thus, as he concluded, "it's preposterous to think that if he had appeared to them in that awful state, his followers would have been prompted to start a worldwide movement based on the hope that someday they too would have a resurrection body like his."[5] The inevitable conclusion is that the swoon hypothesis is a leap of faith into a chasm of credulity.

The Major Swoon Flaws

Philosopher and New Testament historian Dr. Gary Habermas dismisses swoon hypotheses for three major reasons. First, as recounted by the apostle John, when the soldiers determined that Jesus was dead, one of them "pierced Jesus' side with a spear, bringing a sudden flow of blood and water" (John 19:34). As a first-century man, John would not likely have known what twentieth-century science has only recently discovered—namely, that blood and water flowed from the side of Jesus due to the fact that the heart is surrounded by a sac of water, called a pericardium. The water came from Christ's pierced pericardium; the blood came from his pierced heart. Says Habermas, "Even if Jesus was alive before he was stabbed, the lance would almost certainly have killed him. Therefore, this chest wound also disproves the swoon theory."[6]

Furthermore, as demonstrated by the nineteenth-century liberal scholar David Strauss, even if Jesus had survived his crucifixion, he could never have rolled a massive tombstone uphill out of its gully—especially in his weakened condition and without so much as an edge against which to push from inside the tomb. Had he accomplished this miraculous feat, he would then have had to limp around on pierced feet, find his disciples' hideout, and then convince them that he had conquered death and the grave. Strauss points out that, far from fantasizing that this bleeding shell of a man was their Savior, the disciples would have run and fetched a doctor.[7] Dr. Habermas notes that Albert Schweitzer referred to Strauss's critique as "the 'death-blow' to such rationalistic approaches. After Strauss's views were circulated, the liberal 'lives of Jesus' usually shunned the swoon hypothesis. By the early twentieth century, other critical scholars proclaimed this hypothesis to be nothing more than a historical curiosity of the past. Even critics no longer considered it to be a viable hypothesis."[8]

Finally, as demonstrated by twentieth-century medical

research, crucifixion is essentially death by asphyxiation. As the body hangs downward, the intercostal and pectoral muscles surrounding the lungs halt the normal process of breathing. Thus, even if Jesus had been given a drug to put him in a deathlike trance, he would not have been able to survive death by asphyxiation. As Habermas puts it, "one cannot fake the inability to breathe for any length of time."[9] The late liberal Cambridge scholar John A. T. Robinson suggested that the swoon hypothesis is so fatally flawed that "if the public were not so interested in virtually anyone who writes on Christianity, it 'would be laughed out of court.'"[10]

Having established the scriptural reliability of Christ's fatal torment, we now turn to the E in the acronym FEAT, which will serve to remind us of the second unshakable pillar undergirding the Resurrection: the empty tomb.

THREE

Empty Tomb

When the Sabbath was over, Mary Magdalene, Mary the mother of James, and Salome bought spices so that they might go to anoint Jesus' body. Very early on the first day of the week, just after sunrise, they were on their way to the tomb and they asked each other, "Who will roll the stone away from the entrance of the tomb?"

But when they looked up, they saw that the stone, which was very large, had been rolled away. As they entered the tomb, they saw a young man dressed in a white robe sitting on the right side, and they were alarmed.

"Don't be alarmed," he said. "You are looking for Jesus the Nazarene, who was crucified. He has risen! He is not here. See the place where they laid him." (Mark 16:1–6)

THE YEAR 1985 MARKED THE BEGINNING of one of the most well-publicized wars in history. This was not a war of weapons; rather, it was a war of words. It began with a coalition of "scholars" who dubbed themselves the Jesus Seminar. These scholars were determined to demolish the biblical Jesus in the public arena, rather than merely in private academia.

They were determined "to liberate the people of the church from the 'dark ages of theological tyranny.' "[1]

Jesus Seminar founder Robert Funk is bent on convincing the world that the historical Jesus is not worthy of worship. Said Funk, "Jesus himself should not be, must not be, the object of faith. That would be to repeat the idolatry of the first believers."[2] His stated objective is "to liberate Jesus. The only Jesus most people know is the mythic one. They don't want the real Jesus, they want the one they can worship. The cultic Jesus."[3] Fellow cofounder John Dominic Crossan took dead aim at the resurrection of Jesus Christ. *Time* magazine reports Crossan's pontification: "The tales of entombment and resurrection were latter-day wishful thinking. Instead, Jesus' corpse went the way of all abandoned criminals' bodies: it was probably barely covered with dirt, vulnerable to the wild dogs that roamed the wasteland of the execution grounds."[4]

The founders of the Jesus Seminar make little attempt to hide their disdain for the biblical Jesus. Crossan denigrates him as "a peasant Jewish cynic," and Funk demeans him as "perhaps the first stand-up Jewish comic."[5] At times, the assertions of Jesus Seminar participants are so outrageous that the eminent Jewish scholar Jacob Neusner called the Jesus Seminar "either the greatest scholarly hoax since the Piltdown Man or the utter bankruptcy of New Testament studies—I hope the former."[6]

Multitudes uncritically accept the assertions of the Jesus Seminar, failing to recognize that they fly in the face of well-established facts. Unlike a consensus of credible scholarship, Jesus Seminar scholars are famous for making dogmatic assertions while failing to provide defensible arguments. For example, they dogmatically assert that Jesus did not say more than 80 percent of what is attributed to him by Matthew, Mark, Luke, and John. This indefensible assertion is based on what theologian Dr. Gregory Boyd described as their own unique brand of fundamentalism.[7] The so-called historical Jesus that has emerged is: (1) nonapocalyptic, (2) socially subversive, (3) a stand-up comic, (4) a mere human, (5) focused on the here-and-now, (6) one who did not intend to organize a following, (7) and one whose death was merely an insignificant accident of history. Thus, according to the Jesus Seminar, belief in the Resurrection was merely a later Christian myth.[8]

In short, the fellows of the Jesus Seminar begin with an anti-supernatural bias and thus reject the Resurrection *a priori* (prior to empirical examination). In place of reason and evidential substance, they offer rhetoric and emotional stereotypes. Those who disagree with their presuppositions are stereotypically regarded as intellectually retarded and reduced to residing in the Dark Ages. If the Jesus Seminar fellows are anything, they are media savvy. They have attracted huge headlines by painting evangelicals as naive fundamentalists who uncritically buy into the biblical account of the empty tomb. Using colored beads in a ballot vote, they reject the authenticity of statements attributed to Christ by the Gospel writers. In their view, red beads, black beads, and pink beads mean "yes," "no," and "maybe so," respectively. As an intermediate category, they use gray beads to designate words that "did not originate with Jesus though they may reflect his ideas."[9] In their view, fewer than 20 percent of Christ's sayings are credible.

Jesus Seminar participants clearly loathe the Gospel of John and love the Gospel of Thomas—this despite the fact that Thomas includes such patently ignorant and politically incorrect passages as the following conversation between Peter and Jesus: "Simon Peter said to them, 'Make Mary leave us, for females don't deserve life.' Jesus said, 'Look, I will guide her to make her male, so that she too may become a living spirit resembling you males. For every female who makes herself male will enter the domain of Heaven.'"[10]

The *Christian Research Journal* notes that when the Jesus Seminar released their color-coded "scholars version" of *The Five Gospels* in 1993, the second-century Gospel of Thomas was thrust into prime time: "For all intents and purposes, the Jesus Seminar has 'canonized' this 'Gospel,' known primarily from a Coptic translation found in Egypt at Nag Hammadi in late 1945. . . . In fact, it is quite clear that the scholars of the Seminar consider the Gospel of Thomas far more reliable and important than the Gospel of John, and probably more than Matthew and Luke's Gospels as well, as far as being useful in 'reconstructing' the words of the 'historical Jesus.'"[11]

Even a cursory reading of the Gospel of Thomas should suffice to see how deeply it was influenced by second-century gnostic concepts that came in vogue long after the New Testament period.[12] Yet the Jesus Seminar speculates that the Gospel of Thomas is earlier and more authentic than the biblical accounts.[13] Christian philosopher and theologian William Lane Craig lamented, "It is sobering to think that it is this sort of idiosyncratic speculation that thousands of lay readers of magazines like *Time* have come to believe represents the best of contemporary New Testament scholarship."[14]

As the reliability of the Resurrection is undermined in the

media, it is crucial that Christians are prepared to demonstrate that Jesus was buried and that, on Easter morning some two thousand years ago, the tomb was indeed empty. Contrary to Crossan, the late liberal scholar John A. T. Robinson of Cambridge conceded that the burial of Christ "is one of the earliest and best-attested facts about Jesus."[15] This statement is not merely a dogmatic assertion, but rather stands firmly upon sound argumentation.

The Fictional Pharisee Fallacy

Liberal and conservative New Testament scholars alike agree that the body of Jesus was buried in the private tomb of Joseph of Arimathea. Craig underscores this fact by noting that, as a member of the Jewish court that condemned Jesus, Joseph of Arimathea is unlikely to be Christian fiction. The noted New Testament scholar Raymond Brown explains that "Joseph's being responsible for burying Jesus is 'very probable,' since a Christian fictional creation of a Jewish Sanhedrist doing what is right for Jesus is 'almost inexplicable,' given the hostility toward the Jewish leaders responsible for Jesus' death in early Christian writings. In particular, Mark would not have invented Joseph in view of his statements that the whole

Sanhedrin voted for Jesus' condemnation (Mark 14:55, 64; 15:1)."[16]

Furthermore, no competing burial story exists. Craig points out that "if the burial of Jesus in the tomb by Joseph of Arimathea is legendary, then it is strange that conflicting traditions nowhere appear, even in Jewish polemic. That no remnant of the true story or even a conflicting false one should remain is hard to explain unless the Gospel account is substantially the true account."[17] Additionally, it should be noted that "during Jesus' time there was an extraordinary interest in the graves of Jewish martyrs and holy men, and these were scrupulously cared for and honored. . . . This was so because the bones of the prophet lay in the tomb and imparted to the site its religious value. If the remains were not there, then the grave would lose its significance as a shrine." And in the case of Christ, there is no evidence that the tomb was venerated.[18]

Finally, the account of Jesus' burial in the tomb of Joseph of Arimathea is substantiated by Mark's Gospel and is, therefore, far too early to have been the subject of legendary corruption.[19] Likewise, Paul substantiates Christ's burial in a letter to the Corinthian Christians, in which he recites an ancient Christian creed dating to within a few years of the Crucifixion itself (see 1 Corinthians 15:3–7).[20]

THE FEMALE FACTOR

As Lee Strobel notes in *The Case for Christ,* "when you understand the role of women in first-century Jewish society, what's really extraordinary is that this empty tomb story should feature females as the discoverers of the empty tomb."[21] In fact, "any later legendary account would have certainly portrayed male disciples as discovering the tomb—Peter or John, for example. The fact that women are the first witnesses to the empty tomb is most plausibly explained by the reality that—like it or not—they were the discoverers of the empty tomb! This shows that the gospel writers faithfully recorded what happened, even if it was embarrassing."[22]

To begin with, it should be noted that females were not even allowed to serve as legal witnesses. Says Craig, their testimony "was regarded as so worthless that they could not even testify in a court of law. If a man committed a crime and was observed in the very act by some women, he could not be convicted on the basis of their testimony, since their testimony was regarded as so worthless that it was not even admitted into court."[23]

Furthermore, Craig notes that "women occupied a low rung on the Jewish social ladder. Compared to men, women were second-class citizens. Consider these Jewish texts: 'Sooner let the words of the Law be burnt than delivered to women!' and again: 'Happy is he whose children are male, but unhappy is he whose children are female!'"[24] Prior to the coming of Christ, women were so denigrated by society that "one of the Jewish prayers dated from that era declared, 'I thank thee that I am not a woman.'"[25]

Finally, if Jesus had been a typical Jewish sage, he would not have encouraged women to be his disciples. While women served as maids and mothers in Jewish society, they would never have been allowed to follow a Jewish master as disciples. Even the Greek philosophers of the day were reticent to count women as their disciples. As Craig Keener notes in *The IVP Bible Background Commentary,* for "women to travel with the group would have been viewed as scandalous. Adult coeducation was unheard of, and that these women are learning Jesus' teaching as closely as his male disciples would surely bother some outsiders as well."[26] According to *Nelson's New Illustrated Bible Dictionary,* however, Christ's example and teachings radically challenged the cultural norms:

He invited women to accompany Him and His disciples on their journeys (Luke 8:1–3). He talked with the Samaritan woman at Jacob's Well and led her to a conversion experience (John 4). Jesus did not think it strange that Mary sat at His feet, assuming the role of a disciple; in fact, He suggested to Martha that she should do likewise (Luke 10:38–42). Although the Jews segregated the women in both Temple and synagogue, the early church did not separate the congregation by sex (Acts 12:1–17; 1 Corinthians 11:2–16). The apostle Paul wrote, "there is neither Jew nor Greek, there is neither slave nor free, there is neither male nor female; for you are all one in Christ Jesus." (Galatians 3:28)[27]

THE FIRST RESPONSE

Finally, as Craig emphasizes in *Jesus Under Fire,* the earliest Jewish response to the resurrection of Jesus Christ presupposes the empty tomb. Instead of denying that the tomb was empty, the antagonists of Christ accused his disciples of stealing the body. Their response to the proclamation "He has risen—He is risen indeed" was not "His body is still in the tomb," or "He was thrown into a shallow grave and eaten by dogs." Instead, they responded, "His disciples came during the night and stole him away" (Matthew 28:13).[28] In the centuries following the Resurrection, the fact of the empty tomb was forwarded by Jesus' friends and foes alike.

The medieval Jewish polemic *Toledot Yeshu* not only states that Jesus suffered fatal torment but sings the common chorus, "His disciples came during the night and stole him away." In this fifth-century version of the Passover plot hypothesis, a gardener named Juda discovers the disciples' devious plan to steal the body of Jesus. Beating them to the punch, he robs Jesus from the tomb of Joseph and disposes of his body in a freshly dug grave. He then tells the foes of Christ what he had done and offers them the body of the Savior for thirty pieces of silver. The Jewish leaders bought the cadaver and subsequently dragged it through the streets of the city in evidence that Christ had not risen from the dead as he said he would.[29]

While this fanciful story has no historical merit, it underscores the earliest evidence extant—the empty tomb! In short, early Christianity simply could not have survived an identifiable tomb containing the corpse of Christ. The enemies of Christ could have easily put an end to the charade by displaying the body as depicted in *Toledot Yeshu*. Even Jesus Seminar founder John Dominic Crossan would be forced by the facts to concede that no one can affirm the historicity of Christ's burial while simultaneously denying the historicity of the empty tomb.[30]

Having demonstrated that the empty tomb is an unassailable reality, we now turn to the letter A in the acronym FEAT, which will serve to remind us of the third unshakable pillar supporting the Resurrection—namely, the postresurrection appearances of Christ.

FOUR

Appearances of Christ

Jesus himself stood among them and said to them, "Peace be with you." They were startled and frightened, thinking they saw a ghost. He said to them, "Why are you troubled, and why do doubts rise in your minds? Look at my hands and my feet. It is I myself! Touch me and see; a ghost does not have flesh and bones, as you see I have." (Luke 24:36–39)

IN THE BOOK OF ACTS, Dr. Luke writes that Jesus gave the disciples "many convincing proofs that he was alive. He appeared to them over a period of forty days and spoke about the kingdom of God" (Acts 1:3). Likewise, Peter in his powerful Pentecost proclamation confidently communicated that many credible eyewitnesses could confirm the fact of Christ's physical postresurrection appearances: "Brothers, I can tell you confidently that the patriarch David died and was buried, and his tomb is here to this day. But he was a prophet and knew that God had promised him on oath that he would place one of his descendants on his throne. Seeing what was ahead, he spoke of the resurrection of the Christ, that he was not abandoned to the grave, nor did his body see decay. God has raised this Jesus to life, and we are all witnesses of the fact" (Acts 2:29–32).

Like the apostle Peter, the apostle Paul exudes confidence in the appearances of Christ. In his first letter to the Corinthian Christians, he provides details and descriptions:

> Now, brothers, I want to remind you of the gospel I preached to you, which you received and on which you have taken your stand. By this gospel you are saved, if you hold firmly to the word I preached to you. Otherwise, you have believed in vain.
>
> For what I received I passed on to you as of first importance: that Christ died for our sins according to the Scriptures, that he was buried, that he was raised on the third day according to the Scriptures, and that he appeared to Peter, and then to the Twelve. After that, he appeared to more than five hundred of the brothers at the same time, most of whom are still living, though some have fallen asleep. Then he appeared to James, then to all the apostles, and last of all he appeared to me also, as to one abnormally born. (1 Corinthians 15:1–8)

EARLIEST CHRISTIAN CREED

One thing can be stated with iron-clad certainty: The apostles did not merely propagate Christ's teachings; they were absolutely positive that he had appeared to them in the flesh. Although we are now two thousand years removed from the actual event, we too can be absolutely confident in Christ's postresurrection appearances. One of the principal reasons for this confidence is that, within the passage cited above (1 Corinthians 15:3–7), Paul is reiterating a Christian creed that can be traced all the way back to the formative stages of the early Christian church.[1] Incredibly, scholars of all stripes agree that this creed can be dated to within three to eight years of the Crucifixion itself.[2] In his seminal work titled *The Historical Jesus: Ancient Evidence for the Life of Christ,* Dr. Gary Habermas lists a variety of reasons by which scholars have come to this conclusion.

First, Paul employs technical Jewish terminology used to transmit oral tradition when he uses such words as *delivered* and *received.* Scholars view this as evidence that Paul is reciting information he received from another source. The eminent scholar Joachim Jeremias, a leading authority on this issue, also points to non-Pauline phrases such as *for our sins* (v. 3), *according to the Scriptures* (vv. 3, 4), *he was raised* (v. 4), *third day* (v. 4), *he appeared* (vv. 5, 6, 7, 8), and *the Twelve* (v. 5). Furthermore, "the creed is organized in a stylized, parallel form" that reflects an oral tradition. And finally, Paul's use of the Aramaic word *Cephas* for Peter points to an extremely early Semitic source.[3]

Oxford scholar and philosopher Dr. Terry Miethe concurs: "Most New Testament scholars point out that one of the ways we know [1 Corinthians 15:3–7] is a creedal statement is that it appears to have been in a more primitive Aramaic, and it's also in hymnic form. This means it was stylized Greek, non-Pauline words, and so on, which indicates that it predated Paul and was widely used, probably even used and recited in worship experiences as a form of worship or a song or a hymn or a creedal statement, and was therefore universally acknowledged."[4]

The enormous implications of the early dating of this creed can hardly be overstated. Jeremias refers to it as "'the earliest tradition of all,' and Ulrich Wilckens says it 'indubitably goes back to the oldest phase of all in the history of primitive Christianity.'"[5] Greco-Roman classical historian A. N. Sherwin-White argues that it would be unprecedented historically for legend to have grown up that fast.[6] He points out that the sources used for Greek and Roman history are not only biased, but generations or even centuries removed from the actual events they chronicle. Nonetheless, these sources are the basis on which historians confidently reconstruct the historical facts concerning Greek and Roman history.[7]

Dr. William Lane Craig points out that the writings of Herodotus[8] provide us with a perspective on the rate at which legend accumulates—the data demonstrates that even two generations is insufficient for embellishments to supplant a specific set of historical facts. The short time span between Christ's crucifixion and the composition of this early Christian creed precludes the possibility of legendary corruption.[9] Legends draw from folklore, not from people and places that are demonstrably rooted in history. Nineteenth-century scholar Julius Müller underscores this truth in the eloquence of post-Elizabethan English:

> Most decidedly must a considerable interval of time be required for such a complete transformation of a whole history by popular tradition, when the series of legends are formed in the same territory where the heroes actually lived and wrought. Here one cannot imagine how such a series of legends could

arise in an historical age, obtain universal respect, and supplant the historical recollection of the true character and connexion of their heroes' lives in the minds of the community, if eyewitnesses were still at hand, who could be questioned respecting the truth of the recorded marvels. Hence, legendary fiction, as it likes not the clear present time, but prefers the mysterious gloom of grey antiquity, is wont to seek a remoteness of age, along with that of space, and to remove its boldest and most rare and wonderful creations into a very remote and unknown land.[10]

As noted by Craig, Müller "challenged scholars of the mid-nineteenth century to show anywhere in history where within thirty years a great series of legends had accumulated around a historical individual and had become firmly fixed in general belief. *Müller's challenge has never been met.*"[11] It is mind-boggling to realize that Christianity can confidently point to a creed that some of the greatest scholars, theologians, philosophers, and historians have traced to within just three to eight years of Christ's crucifixion. Dr. Gary Habermas makes it crystal-clear that we should never "undermine the persuasive evidence that the creed is early, that it's free from legendary contamination, that it's unambiguous and specific, and that it's ultimately rooted in eyewitness accounts."[12]

EYEWITNESSES

Peter, Paul, and the rest of the apostles claimed that Christ appeared to hundreds of people who were still alive and available for cross-examination.[13] For example, Paul claims that Christ "appeared to more than five hundred of the brothers at the same time, most of whom are still living, though some have fallen asleep" (1 Corinthians 15:6). It would have been one thing to attribute these supernatural experiences to people who had already died. It was quite another to attribute them to multitudes who were still alive.

As the famed New Testament scholar of Cambridge University C. H. Dodd points out, "There can hardly be any purpose in mentioning the fact that most of the five hundred are still alive, unless Paul is saying, in effect, 'The witnesses are there to be questioned.'"[14] Says Craig, "Paul could never have said this if the event had never occurred; he could never have challenged people to ask the witnesses if the event had not taken place and there were no witnesses. But evidently there were witnesses to this event, and Paul knew that some had died in the meantime. Therefore, the event must have taken place."[15]

Suppose I announced publicly that I played a private round of golf with Arnold Palmer at Bay Hill Country Club in Orlando. During the round I hit the longest drive Palmer had ever seen, made a hole-in-one, and set a new course record. As long as Palmer was living, my credibility could easily be called into question. Likewise, Paul's assertions regarding the eyewitnesses who had seen the resurrected Christ could have easily been refuted if in fact they were not true.

Furthermore, nothing can account for the utter transformation of Paul on the road to Damascus other than the appearance of Christ. While he was yet "breathing out murderous threats against the Lord's disciples," Christ appeared to him. "Suddenly a light from heaven flashed around him. He fell to the ground and heard a voice say to him, 'Saul, Saul, why do you persecute me?'" (Acts 9:1, 3–4). In that instant Paul was transformed from a persecutor of Christians to a proselytizer for Christ. He had once approvingly watched as Stephen was brutally murdered; now he was willing to be murdered for the same Christian testimony. Only the appearance of Christ can account for that.

Incredibly, Paul gave up his position as an esteemed Jewish leader, a rabbi, and a Pharisee who had studied under the famed teacher Gamaliel. He gave up the mission to stamp out every vestige of what he considered the insidious heresy of Christianity. In his words, "I persecuted the church of God and tried to destroy it" (Galatians 1:13). But after the resurrected Christ appeared to him, he became as committed to the gospel as he had been to Gamaliel. In his second letter to the Corinthian Christians, he outlines how he traded in his position as a Pharisee for poverty, prison, and persecution (see 2 Corinthians 11:23–28).

Paul was no doubt the most radically converted man in history. In the end, he paid the ultimate price for his faith—martyrdom. The stone inscription beneath the high altar at St. Paul's Basilica in Rome simply reads, "To Paul, Apostle and Martyr."[16] Only the physical appearance of the resurrected Christ is a sufficient explanation for such a radical transformation.

Finally, it should be noted that Christ's appearances to Paul and the five hundred are not isolated incidences. As noted by Craig, Paul provides a list of Christ's appearances in 1 Corinthians 15:5–7.[17] Among them is his appearance to

Peter—which is vouched for by Peter himself (see 2 Peter 1:16). Dr. Luke adds confirmation to this appearance, "saying, 'It is true!' The Lord has risen and has appeared to Simon" (Luke 24:34). Perhaps the most well-attested appearance of all is Christ's appearance to the Twelve. Independent attestations of this appearance are provided by both Luke and John, who recount Christ's eating with the Twelve and showing them his wounds (see Luke 24:36–43; John 20:19–20). Thus, Jesus not only demonstrated "that he was the *same Jesus* who had been crucified," but provided proof for the "*corporeality* and *continuity* of the resurrection body."[18]

No doubt the most amazing appearance listed by Paul is Christ's appearance to his half brother, James. Before this appearance, James was embarrassed by Jesus. Afterward, James was willing to die for Jesus. As the Jewish historian Josephus reports, "James was stoned to death illegally by the Sanhedrin sometime after A.D. 60 for his faith in Christ."[19] Inevitably, you have to ask yourself the question, What would it take for a person to die willingly for the belief that one of his family members is God? In the case of James, the only reasonable explanation is that Jesus appeared to him alive from the dead.[20] Says Craig, "even the skeptical NT critic Hans Grass admits that the conversion of James is one of the surest proofs of the resurrection of Jesus Christ."[21]

EXTREME MEASURES

Since reason and rhetoric cannot dispense with the Resurrection, extreme measures are often the order of the day. Unable to explain away the many physical appearances of Christ, critics are often reduced to explaining them away as merely psychological appearances. Thus, it is argued that the devotees of Christ may well have been experiencing hallucinations, hypnosis, or hypersuggestibility.

HALLUCINATION HYPOTHESIS

The hallucination hypothesis must surely rank as one of the most extreme measures used to explain away the postresurrection appearances of Christ. According to this hypothesis, the disciples merely saw things they wanted to see as the result of extravagances ranging from drug use to expectations. The arguments of resurrection critics are fairly straightforward: If devotees of Christianity throughout history have experienced hallucinations, there is reason to think that the disciples of Christ experienced hallucinations as well.

Here's how philosopher and atheist Dr. Michael Martin tells the story. Says Martin, we "know from the history of witchcraft that people who are thought to be bewitched had hallucinations that caused those around them to have hallucinations also. For example, Cotton Mather told the story of Mercy Short, a seventeen-year-old Boston servant girl who, in 1692, was cursed by Sarah Good, 'a hag.' Thinking herself bewitched, Mercy started to exhibit various symptoms, including hallucinations of groups of specters."[22] Martin goes on to note another occasion during which Mercy had a hallucination. This time she saw spectral fire. "Mather reported that 'we saw not the flames, but once the room smelled of brimstone.'" Thus, according to Martin:

It seems clear that in the context of seventeenth-century New England, where witches and demons were taken for granted, one person's hallucination somehow triggered visual, auditory, tactile, and olfactory hallucinations in those nearby. Surely, it is not beyond the realm of psychological possibility, as [Gary] Habermas seems to assume it is, that in first-century Palestine, among the unsophisticated people who believed in the divinity of Jesus, one disciple's hallucination of Jesus could have triggered corresponding hallucinations in the others. The context, background, and psychological state of the disciples were no less congenial to this sort of collective hallucination than those of the people in Salem or in Boston about three hundred years ago.[23]

Those, like Martin, who use the hallucination hypothesis as a possible explanation for the postresurrection appearances of Christ are just as likely to point to current examples of Christian gullibility—such as a hallucination that took place at a Rick Joyner conference, during which participants sang one song "for over three hours."[24] As a result, Joyner said, "the gulf between heaven and earth had somehow been bridged."[25] He went on to report that when that one song finally ended, some of the musicians were lying on the floor: "I looked at Christine Potter and Susy Wills, who were dancing near the center of the stage and I have never seen such a look of terror on the faces of anyone. An intense burning, like a nuclear fire that burns from the inside out, seemed to be on the stage. Christine started pulling at her clothes as if she were on fire, and Susy dove behind the drums. Then a cloud appeared on the center of the stage, visible to everyone, and a sweet smell like flowers filled the area."[26]

While critics of Christianity, such as Michael Martin, may point to examples like those cited above, their attempts to explain away the postresurrection appearances of Christ as hallucinations do not stand up in the cold, hard light of facts. First, in sharp distinction to Michael Martin's contention that hallucinations are common and contagious, in reality they are subjective and scarce. Yet Christ appeared to many people during a long period of time. As noted by psychologist Dr. Gary Collins, "Hallucinations are individual occurrences. By their very nature only one person can see a given hallucination at a time. They certainly aren't something which can be seen by a group of people. Neither is it possible that one person could somehow induce a hallucination in somebody else. Since an hallucination exists only in this subjective, personal sense, it is obvious that others cannot witness it."[27]

Dr. Collins goes on to assert that for someone to prove that the disciples were hallucinating when they experienced the resurrected Christ, "they would have to go against much of the current psychiatric and psychological data about the nature of hallucinations."[28] Thus, the incontrovertible fact that Christ appeared to multitudes on multiple occasions poses an enormous enigma for hallucination theorists.

Furthermore, hallucinations are typically relegated to people with certain personality disorders, are stimulated by expectations, and do not stop abruptly. However, Christ appeared to all kinds of personality types with no expectations, and then the appearances ceased. As Dr. Habermas points out:

> Hallucinations can't explain away his appearances. . . .
> The disciples were fearful, doubtful, and in despair after the Crucifixion, whereas people who hallucinate need a fertile mind of expectancy or anticipation. Peter was hardheaded, for goodness' sake; James was a skeptic—certainly not good candidates for hallucinations. Also, hallucinations are comparably rare. They're usually caused by drugs or bodily deprivation. Chances are, you don't know anybody who's ever had a hallucination not caused by one of those two things. Yet we're supposed to believe that over a course of many weeks, people from all sorts of backgrounds, all kinds of temperaments, in various places, all experienced hallu-

cinations? That strains the hypothesis quite a bit, doesn't it? Besides, if we establish the gospel accounts as being reliable, how do you account for the disciples eating with Jesus and touching him? How does he walk along with two of them on the road to Emmaus? And what about the empty tomb? If people only thought they saw Jesus, his body would still be in his grave.[29]

One final point should be made: Hallucinations in and of themselves would not have led to a belief in resurrection on the part of the disciples. Craig explains that hallucinations, "as projections of the mind, can contain nothing new. Therefore, given the current Jewish beliefs about life after death, the disciples would have projected hallucinations of Jesus in heaven or in Abraham's bosom, where the souls of the righteous dead were believed to abide until the resurrection. And such visions would not have caused belief in Jesus' resurrection."[30] The inevitable conclusion, says Craig, is that hallucinations might have led the disciples to believe that Jesus had been *translated,* but not that he had been *resurrected* from the dead:

Translation is the bodily assumption of someone out of this world into heaven. Resurrection is the raising up of a dead man in the space-time universe. Thus, given Jewish beliefs concerning translation and resurrection, the disciples would not have preached that Jesus had been raised from the dead. At the very most, the empty tomb and hallucinations of Jesus would have only caused them to believe in the translation of Jesus, for this fit in with their Jewish frame of thought. But they would not have come up with the idea that Jesus had been raised from the dead, for this contradicted the Jewish belief.[31]

HYPNOSIS HYPOTHESIS

Another extreme measure employed by critics of the Resurrection is the hypnosis hypothesis.[32] This is the notion that the disciples were in some sort of an altered state of consciousness as a result of sleep deprivation or suffocating despair over the loss of their Master. Dr. Charles Tart, credited with coining the term *altered states of consciousness,* explained that during deep hypnosis a person transitions to a new state of consciousness, which causes him or her to lose touch with reality.[33] As has been well documented from studies of the world of the occult, the dangerous effects of hypnosis may involve depression, detachment, depersonalization, disillusionment, and many equally serious disorders.[34]

As underscored by hypnosis researcher Robert W. Marks, "people in crowds are more easily influenced than people taken singly. This fact has been capitalized on by stage hypnotists as well as evangelists, political orators, and dictators."[35] Says Marks, "the effect of suggestion on crowds seems virtually without limit. It can make black appear white. It can obscure realities, enshrine absurdities, and impel men pitilessly to cleave the skulls of their brothers."[36] Marks also notes that once epidemic suggestion contaminates a movement, human beings can "behave like beasts or idiots and be proud of it."[37] No one "is immune to the force of mass suggestion. Once an epidemic of hysteria is in full force it strikes intellectuals as well as morons, rich and poor alike. Its well-springs are subconscious and biological, not rational."[38] Under mass hypnosis, devotees of a movement can become extremely susceptible to spontaneous suggestions. Researcher Charles Baudouin writes, "a condition of mental relaxation is imposed upon the participants. Secondly, an emotional state is invariably aroused by approximation to the mysterious. Thirdly, there exists an expectation that remarkable things will happen."[39]

A classic case in point can be found in the story of a young Bronx boy named Joseph Vitolo.[40] In his book *The Story of Hypnosis,* Marks recounts that in 1945, nine-year-old Joseph was kneeling on a rock in an empty lot when he saw a vision of the Virgin Mary. Mary promised Joseph that she would appear on successive nights and that on the night of her last appearance, a miraculous spring would emerge from the ground.

Following the announcement, crowds trekked to the scene of the alleged vision. On one night, twenty-five thousand people surged to the scene with flowers, candles, and statues of saints. It was automatically assumed that Joseph had a special anointing. Thus, dozens of the disabled were brought to Joseph so that he would lay hands on them.

While Joseph was not able to accomplish anything out of the ordinary, the expectations of the crowd were such that they began to create their own "miracles." On one of the nights, a light rain began to fall, and a woman screamed, "It's pouring, yet Joseph doesn't get wet." Despite the fact that news reporters standing near Joseph observed that he was as soaked as anyone else, the expectations of the miraculous created the illusion. Another woman claimed she saw an apparition in white materialize behind Joseph. In reality, the apparition was nothing more than another woman protectively covered with a white raincoat.

Marks points out that the expectations of the crowd were such that "if imagination and hysterical contagion had been left to do their hallucinatory work, the crowd would have created its own miracle. And it is highly probable that Joseph could have produced some real 'cures' and real 'visions' if the hypnotic effects of the situation could have progressed far enough."[41] The expectations of the crowd had been heightened to such an extent that, as Marks says, they were "no more capable of resisting the proper hypnotic suggestion than Pavlov's dog was capable of resisting the stimulus to salivate."[42]

Skeptics of the Resurrection suggest that this may very well have been what happened to the followers of Christ. In a highly suggestible hypnotic state, the disciples saw what they wanted to see—the appearance of Jesus in the flesh! This notion, however, is completely ad hoc—in other words, there is not a shred of evidence to substantiate it. While it is true that spiritual leaders, political orators, and dictators have capitalized on crowd dynamics to fool the masses, there is no warrant for suggesting that this is what happened to the disciples. The hypnotic hypothesis has been dogmatically asserted by antisupernaturalists, but no one has ever presented a defensible argument to substantiate it. As demonstrated conclusively, the disciples did not just proliferate Christ's teachings; they were absolutely positive that he had risen from the dead.

Further, there is no warrant for believing that the disciples were in the practice of working themselves into altered states of consciousness. Even a cursory reading of the writings of the apostles demonstrates that they had a high regard for the mind. Far from seeking to dull the critical-thinking process, they exhorted one another to be alert and sober-minded (see 1 Thessalonians 5:6; 1 Peter 5:8). If there is any doubt that the disciples were committed to reason, one reading of the book of Romans will forever erase that doubt.

Hindu gurus like Baghwan Shree Rajneesh believed the "goal is to create a new man, one who is happily mindless."[43] Thus, he engaged his devotees in practices designed to subjugate their critical-thinking faculties and empty their minds of coherent thought. In sharp distinction, the Judeo-Christian tradition has a high view of the mind. In the Old Testament, the Israelites were instructed to practice good judgment through inquiring, probing, and thoroughly investigating a teaching and practice (see Deuteronomy 13). Likewise, in the New

Testament, the apostle Paul commands the Thessalonians to "test everything" (1 Thessalonians 5:21) and commends the Bereans for using their minds to analyze his teachings in light of an objective frame of reference—Scripture (see Acts 17:11). The Master himself commanded the disciples to judge rightly (see John 7:24) and to love God with all of their hearts, souls, and minds (see Matthew 22:37). Thus, while hypnotism is capitalized on frequently in aberrant Christianity and in the kingdom of the cults, it is completely foreign to the kingdom of Christ.

Finally, as underscored by theologian and historian Carl Braaten, "Even the more skeptical historians agree that for primitive Christianity . . . the resurrection of Jesus from the dead was a real event in history, the very foundation of faith, and not a mythical idea arising out of the creative imagination of believers."[44] It is an established historical fact that Jesus was fatally tormented, that he was buried, that his tomb was indeed empty three days later, and that Christ's postresurrection appearances were a material reality so certain that the disciples were willing to die for it.

Hypersuggestibility Hypothesis

One final extreme measure should be considered before

moving on—namely, the hypersuggestibility hypothesis. This is the basic idea that the disciples were by nature highly suggestible and thus susceptible to creating the postresurrection appearances of Christ out of thin air and then believing them. It is suggested that under the influence of an eastern guru like Jesus, devotees are apt to set aside their ability to think rationally or to exercise their wills. Thus, they become hypersuggestible, "which means that they are likely to accept any 'spiritual truth' that enters their minds. Even more remarkably, they seem to be primed for mystical experiences and may attach great spiritual significance to virtually any event or thought, no matter how mundane or outlandish."[45]

Such fantasy proneness on the part of the disciples is typically referred to as "Grade Five Syndrome."[46] While Grade Five personalities may well be intuitive and intelligent, they also have vivid, visual imaginations. Thus, they are highly susceptible to the power of suggestion. To begin with, they are very trusting. Second, they desire to please (particularly an authority figure, such as Jesus). Third, they have the capacity to accept contradictory experiences. Fourth, they have a marked propensity for affiliation with new or unusual events. Fifth, they are apt to relate everything to their own self-perception.[47]

This complex of characteristics makes Grade Five personalities particularly susceptible to spiritual fantasies, "psychic and out-of-body experiences, and the occasional difficulty of differentiating fantasized events and persons from nonfantasized ones."[48] It is reasoned that if one out of twelve Americans is susceptible to such fantasy proneness,[49] then perhaps it is not unreasonable to believe that a mere twelve disciples could fall into this category as well.

In responding to the notion that the disciples were merely hypersuggestible and thus uncritically accepted the postresurrection appearances of Christ, Dr. Luke comes immediately to mind. Says Luke, "Many have undertaken to draw up an account of the things that have been fulfilled among us, just as they were handed down to us by those who from the first were eyewitnesses and servants of the word. Therefore, since I myself have carefully investigated everything from the beginning, it seemed good also to me to write an orderly account for you, most excellent Theophilus, so that you may know the certainty of the things you have been taught" (Luke 1:1–4).

A cursory reading of Luke's Gospel or his Acts is sufficient to demonstrate that he was anything but "Grade Five." Far from hypersuggestible, Dr. Luke was committed to history. Thus, he

"carefully investigated" the details surrounding the postresurrection appearances of Christ. In a debate with atheist and philosopher
Dr. Antony Flew, Dr. Habermas exploded the contention that the
disciples were little more than hypersuggestible visionaries.
Cutting through Flew's rhetoric with rigorous reason, Habermas
demonstrated why a preponderance of "critical historians,
philosophers, theologians, and scripture scholars" have universally
accepted the following core set of facts:

> The key evidence for Jesus' resurrection is (1) the
> disciples' eyewitness experiences, which they believed
> to be literal appearances of the risen Jesus; these expe-
> riences have not been explained by naturalistic theo-
> ries, and additional facts corroborate this eyewitness
> testimony. Other positive evidences include (2) the
> early proclamation of the Resurrection by these
> eyewitnesses, (3) their transformation into bold
> witnesses who were willing to die for their convic-
> tions, (4) the empty tomb, and (5) the fact that the
> Resurrection of Jesus was the center of the apostolic
> message, all of which require adequate explanations. It
> is also found that the disciples proclaimed this message

in Jerusalem itself, where it is related that in repeated confrontations with the authorities, (6) the Jewish leaders could not disprove their message even though they had both the power and the motivation to do so.

Additionally, (7) the very existence of the church, founded by monotheistic, law-abiding Jews who nonetheless (8) worshiped on Sunday demand historical causes as well.

Two additionally strong facts arguing for the historicity of the Resurrection are that two skeptics, (9) James and (10) Paul, became Christians after having experiences that they also believed were appearances of the risen Jesus.[50]

No one summed up the consensus of both liberal and conservative scholarship better than Professor Norman Perrin, the late New Testament scholar at the University of Chicago: *"The more we study the tradition with regard to the appearances, the firmer the rock begins to appear upon which they are based."*[51]

At this point, there should be no doubt that Christ suffered fatal torment, that the empty tomb is a factual reality, and that Christ's postresurrection appearances cannot be explained away by legends or extreme measures. Thus, we now move on to the final letter in the acronym FEAT, which represents the word *transformation*. There we will underscore the fact that, far from being fantasy-prone, the disciples were fearless proselytizers who transformed the world because they had encountered the living, resurrected Christ.

f i v e

Transformation

Whatever was to my profit I now consider loss
for the sake of Christ. (Philippians 3:7)

W HAT HAPPENED as a result of the Resurrection is unprecedented in human history. In the span of a few hundred years, a small band of seemingly insignificant believers succeeded in turning an entire empire upside down. As has been well said, "they faced the tyrant's brandished steel, the lion's gory mane, and the fires of a thousand deaths,"[1] because they were utterly convinced that they, like their Master, would one day rise from the grave in glorified, resurrected bodies.

While it is conceivable that the disciples would have faced torture, vilification, and even cruel deaths for what they fervently believed to be true, it is inconceivable that they would have been willing to die for what they knew to be a lie. No one drove that point home more eloquently than did Dr. Simon Greenleaf, the famous Royall Professor of Law at Harvard. Greenleaf was undoubtedly one of the greatest American authorities on common law evidence of the nineteenth century. His tome titled *A Treatise on the Law of Evidence* is still considered to be one of the most significant works on legal evidence in existence. In 1846, he wrote in *The Testimony of the Evangelists:*

> The great truths which the apostles declared were that Christ had risen from the dead, and that only through repentance from sin, and faith in Him, could men hope for salvation. This doctrine they asserted with one voice, everywhere, not only under the greatest discouragements, but in the face of the most appalling terrors that can be presented to the mind of man.
>
> Their master had recently perished as a malefactor, by the sentence of a public tribunal. His religion sought to overthrow the religions of the whole world. The laws of every country were against the teachings of His disciples. The interests and passions

of all the rulers and great men in the world were against them. The fashion of the world was against them.

Propagating this new faith, even in the most inoffensive and peaceful manner, they could expect nothing but contempt, opposition, revilings, bitter persecutions, stripes, imprisonments, torments, and cruel deaths. Yet this faith they zealously did propagate; and all these miseries they endured undismayed, nay, rejoicing.

As one after another was put to a miserable death, the survivors only prosecuted their work with increased vigor and resolution. The annals of military warfare afford scarcely an example of the like heroic constancy, patience, and unblenching courage. They had every possible motive to review carefully the grounds of their faith, and the evidences of the great facts and truths which they asserted and these motives were pressed upon their attention with the most melancholy and terrific frequency. It was therefore impossible that they could have persisted in affirming the truths they have narrated, had not Jesus actually risen from the dead, and had they not known this fact as certainly as they knew any other fact.*

If it were morally possible for them to have been deceived in this matter, every human motive operated to lead them to discover and avow their error. To have persisted in so gross a falsehood, after it was known to them, was not only to encounter, for life, all the evils which man could inflict from without, but to endure also the pangs of inward and conscious guilt; with no hope of future peace, no testimony of a good conscience, no expectation of honor or esteem among men, no hope of happiness in this life, or in the world to come.

Such conduct in the apostles would moreover have been utterly irreconcilable with the fact that they possessed the ordinary constitution of our common nature. Yet their lives do show them to have

---

* *The Testimony of the Evangelists* contains this note: "If the witnesses could be supposed to have been biased, this would not destroy their testimony to matters of fact; it would only detract from the weight of their judgment in matters of opinion. . . ."

been men like all others of our race; swayed by the same motives, animated by the same hopes, affected by the same joys, subdued by the same sorrows, agitated by the same fears, and subject to the same passions, temptations, and infirmities as ourselves. And their writings show them to have been men of vigorous understandings. If then their testimony was not true, there was no possible motive for this fabrication.[2]

THE TWELVE

As Greenleaf so masterfully communicates, the Twelve[3] were thoroughly transformed by the Resurrection.

Peter, who was once afraid of being exposed as a follower of Christ by a young woman, after the Resurrection was transformed into a lion of the faith and suffered a martyr's death.[4] According to tradition, he requested to be crucified upside down, because he felt unworthy to be crucified in the same manner as his Lord.[5]

James, the half brother of Jesus, who once hated everything his brother stood for, after the Resurrection calls himself "a bond-servant . . . of the Lord Jesus Christ" (James 1:1

NASB). He not only became the leader of the Jerusalem church, but in about A.D. 62 was martyred for his faith.[6] Eusebius of Caesarea describes how James was thrown from the pinnacle of the temple and subsequently stoned.[7]

The apostle Paul, likewise, was transformed. Once a ceaseless persecutor of the growing church, he became the chief proselytizer of the Gentiles. His radical transformation is underscored by his letter to the Philippians:

> But whatever was to my profit I now consider loss for the sake of Christ. What is more, I consider everything a loss compared to the surpassing greatness of knowing Christ Jesus my Lord, for whose sake I have lost all things. I consider them rubbish, that I may gain Christ and be found in him, not having a righteousness of my own that comes from the law, but that which is through faith in Christ—the righteousness that comes from God and is by faith. I want to know Christ and the power of his resurrection and the fellowship of sharing in his sufferings, becoming like him in his death, and so, somehow, to attain to the resurrection from the dead. (Philippians 3:7–11)

Peter, James, and Paul were not alone. As Christian philosopher J. P. Moreland points out, within weeks of the Resurrection, not just one, but an entire community of at least ten thousand Jews were willing to give up the very sociological and theological traditions that had given them their national identity.[8]

TRADITIONS

Among the traditions that were transformed after the Resurrection were the Sabbath, the sacrifices, and the sacraments.

In Genesis, the Sabbath was a celebration of God's work in Creation (Genesis 2:2–3; Exodus 20:11). After the Exodus, the Sabbath expanded to a celebration of God's deliverance from the oppression of Egypt (Deuteronomy 5:15). As a result of the Resurrection, the Sabbath shifted once again. It became a celebration of the "rest" we have through Christ who delivers us from sin and the grave (Colossians 2:16–17; Hebrews 4:1–11). In remembrance of the Resurrection, the early Christian church changed the day of worship from the Sabbath to Sunday. God provided the early church with a new pattern of worship through Christ's resurrection on the first day of the week, his subsequent

Sunday appearances, and the Holy Spirit's Sunday descent.[9] For the emerging Christian church, the most dangerous snare was a failure to recognize that Jesus was the substance that fulfilled the symbol of the Sabbath.

For Jewish believers, the sacrificial system was radically transformed by the resurrection of Christ as well. The Jews had been taught from the time of Abraham that they were to sacrifice animals as the symbol of atonement for sin. However, after the Resurrection, the followers of Christ suddenly stopped sacrificing. They recognized that the new covenant was better than the old covenant, because the blood of Jesus Christ was better than the blood of animals (Hebrews 8–10). They finally understood that Jesus was the substance that fulfilled the symbol of animal sacrifices. He was the sacrificial "Lamb of God who takes away the sin of the world" (John 1:29).

Like the Sabbath and the sacrificial system, the Jewish "sacraments" of Passover and baptism were radically transformed. In place of the Passover meal, believers celebrated the Lord's Supper. Moreland points out that Jesus had just been slaughtered in grotesque and humiliating fashion, yet the disciples remembered the broken body and shed blood of Christ with joy. Only the Resurrection can account for that! Imagine devotees of John

F. Kennedy getting together to celebrate his murder at the hands of Lee Harvey Oswald. They may well celebrate his confrontations with communism, his contributions to civil rights, or his captivating charisma, but never his brutal killing.[10]

In like fashion, baptism was radically transformed. Gentile converts to Judaism were baptized in the name of the God of Israel.[11] After the Resurrection, converts to Christianity were baptized in the name of Jesus Christ as well (see Acts 2:36–41).[12] Thus, Christians equated Jesus with Israel's God. Only the Resurrection could account for that.[13]

Today

Each day, people of every tongue and tribe and nation are baptized in the name of the risen Christ. A number of years ago, before the garden tomb in Jerusalem, I encountered a tourist who had no concept of the Resurrection's significance. I explained to him that Christ cloaked himself in human flesh to restore the relationship with God broken by our sin, that Christ lived the perfect life we could never live, and that he died for our sins, was buried, and on the third day rose again from the dead. I went on to explain that this was no mere fantasy but a most well-attested fact of ancient history. After communicating the FEAT that demonstrates the fact of resurrection, this young man took the final step and personally experienced the resurrected Christ. Recognizing that he was a sinner, he repented of his sins and received Jesus Christ as Lord and Savior of his life.

Today he not only knows Christ evidentially, but he knows him experientially as well. Christ has become more real to him than the very flesh upon his bones.

SIX

Resurrection of Believers

To the modern materialist, death is the cessation of being. According to the mythical view of the ancients, when we die we devolve into a ghostly shadow of our present selves. Reincarnationists believe that our souls continuously return dressed up in other bodies. The followers of Plato contend that the body is a prison; at death, the prisoner escapes as a mere individual human spirit. Hindus believe that the body is merely an illusion and that the only thing that ultimately survives is an impersonal cosmic consciousness. Only in a biblical worldview do we become greater after death than we were before. Only in Christianity are our lowly bodies transformed into glorious, resurrected bodies, like unto Christ's resurrected body.[1]

O F ALL THE THINGS THAT CAN BE SAID concerning our glorified bodies, the first and foremost is this: Our lowly bodies will be transformed "like his glorious body" (Philippians 3:21)!

SAVIOR

Like the Savior's body, our resurrection bodies will be real, physical, flesh-and-bone bodies perfectly engineered for "a new heaven and a new earth" (Revelation 21:1). As emphasized by Dr. Norman Geisler, "A resurrected body can be seen with the naked eye. If a picture were taken of it, the image would appear on the film. As Anselm affirmed, it is just as material as Adam's body was and would have remained if Adam had not sinned. It was so physical that were someone to have seen it arise in the tomb, it would have caused dust to fall off the slab from which it arose!"[2]

Furthermore, it is important to note that Christ's resurrection was a historical event that took place in our space-time continuum. Likewise, our resurrection will be a historical event that takes place when Christ physically returns and transforms our mortal bodies in a microsecond. In Paul's words, "we will all be changed—in a flash, in the twinkling of an eye, at the last trumpet. For the trumpet will sound, the dead will be raised imperishable, and we will be changed" (1 Corinthians 15:51–52).

Finally, it should be emphasized that there is a one-to-one correspondence between the body of Christ that died and the body that rose. Jesus said, "Destroy this temple, and I will raise *it* again in three days" (John 2:19; emphasis added). The apostle John clarifies that "the temple he had spoken of was his body"

(v. 21). Says Geisler, "It has always been part of orthodox belief to acknowledge that Jesus was raised immortal in the *same physical body* in which he died. That is, His *resurrection body was numerically the same as his pre-resurrection body.*"[3] Likewise, our resurrection bodies are numerically identical to the bodies we now possess. In other words, our resurrection bodies are not second bodies; rather, they are our present bodies transformed.

SEED

To further inform our thinking with respect to the nature of our resurrected bodies, the apostle Paul provides us with a seed analogy. Says Paul, "But someone may ask, 'How are the dead raised? With what kind of body will they come?' How foolish! What you sow does not come to life unless it dies. When you sow, you do not plant the body that will be, but just a seed, perhaps of wheat or of something else. But God gives it a body as he has determined, and to each kind of seed he gives its own body" (1 Corinthians 15:35–38). As a seed is transformed into the body it will become, so too our mortal bodies will be transformed into the immortal bodies they will be. Joni Eareckson Tada paints a riveting word picture:

Have you ever seen those nature specials on public television? The ones where they put the camera up against a glass to show a dry, old lima bean in the soil? Through time-lapse photography, you watch it shrivel, turn brown, and die. Then, miraculously, the dead shell of that little bean splits open and a tiny lima leg-like root sprouts out. The old bean is shoved aside against the dirt as the little green plant swells. The lima plant came to life because the old bean died.

Not even a Ph.D. in botany can explain how life comes out of death, even in something so simple as a seed. But one thing is for sure: it's a lima bean plant. Not a bush of roses or a bunch of bananas. There's no mistaking it for anything other than what it is. It has absolute identity. Positively, plain as day, a lima bean plant. It may come out of the earth different than when it went in, but it's the same. So it is with the resurrection body. We'll have absolute identification with our body that died.[4]

Much can be gleaned from Paul's seed analogy. First, we see that the blueprints for our glorified bodies are in the bodies we now possess.[5] While orthodoxy does not dictate that every cell of our present bodies will be restored in the resurrection, it does require continuity between our earthly bodies and our heavenly bodies.[6] Just as there is continuity between our present bodies and the bodies we had at birth—even though all of our subatomic particles and most of our cells have been replaced—so too there will be continuity from death to resurrection, despite the fact that not every particle in our bodies will be restored. In fact, without continuity, there is no point in even using the word *resurrection*.

Furthermore, while the blueprints for our glorified bodies are in the bodies we now possess, the blueprints pale by comparison to the buildings they will be—"an eternal house in heaven, not built by human hands" (2 Corinthians 5:1). It would be impossible for a common caterpillar to imagine becoming a beautiful butterfly and soaring off into the wild blue yonder. Likewise, it is impossible for human beings to fully comprehend what we will be capable of in the resurrection.

Finally, it is significant to note that each seed reproduces after its own kind. The DNA for a fetus is not the DNA for a frog, and the DNA for a frog is not the DNA for a fish. Rather, the DNA for a fetus, frog, or fish is uniquely programmed for reproduction after its own kind (see Genesis 1; 1 Corinthians 15:39–44).

SPIRITUAL BODY

The apostle Paul not only wants us to know that our bodies will be transformed like unto our Savior's glorified body and that the seeds of what we will become are in the bodies that we now possess, but he also wants us to know that our natural bodies will be raised spiritual bodies. Some have mistakenly interpreted this to mean that our postresurrection bodies will be ethereal and immaterial. As previously documented, however, nothing could be further from the truth. Christ's resurrection was demonstrably physical. Jesus invited the disciples to examine his resurrected body. He told Thomas, "Put your finger here; see my hands. Reach out your hand and put it into my side. Stop doubting and believe" (John 20:27). The disciples gave Jesus "a piece of broiled fish, and he took it and ate it in their presence" (Luke 24:42–43). And Jesus overtly told the disciples that his body was comprised of "flesh and bones." "Touch me and see," he said. "A ghost does not have flesh and bones, as you see I have" (Luke 24:39).

Dr. Geisler points out that when Paul referred to the "spiritual man" (1 Corinthians 2:15), he did not intend to imply "immaterial man." Rather, he is describing a human being whose life is supernaturally directed by the power of God.[7] Thus "natural man" does not mean "physical man"; it describes a man who is dominated by his sinful human nature. Likewise, "spiritual man" does not mean "nonphysical man," but rather describes a man who is dominated by the supernatural power of the Spirit.

Paul describes the resurrected body as a "spiritual body" in the same sense that we describe the Bible as a "spiritual book."[8] If "spiritual body" means "immaterial body," Satan would have won a strategic battle. God would have had to dispense with our physical nature and re-create humanity as a different ontological species, such as the angels.

In the words of philosopher Peter Kreeft, "It is irrational to suppose we change our species. God does not rip up his handiwork as a mistake. We are created to fill one of the possible levels of reality, one of the unique rungs on the cosmic ladder, between animals and angels. This is our essence, our destiny, and our glory. We would lose that by becoming angels just as much as by becoming apes."[9]

Kreeft further amplifies the significance of physicality in the resurrection by noting that through our natural bodies we can engage in activities of which mere spiritual beings can only dream. Says Kreeft, "We are better than angels at many things, and those things would be missing from us and those perfections missing from the universe if our souls were simply disembodied. Angels are much better than we are at intelligence, will, and power, but they cannot smell flowers or weep over a Chopin nocturne."[10] As Anthony Hoekema concludes: "Then it would indeed seem that matter had become intrinsically evil so that it had to be banished. And then, in a sense, the Greek philosophers would have been proved right. But matter is not evil; it is part of God's good creation. Therefore the goal of God's redemption is the resurrection of the physical body, and the creation of a new earth on which his redeemed people can live and serve God forever with glorified bodies."[11]

Thus, when Paul talks about the "spiritual body" (1 Corinthians 15:44), he is not communicating that we will be re-created as spirit beings, but rather that our resurrected bodies will be supernatural, Spirit dominated, and sin free. First, our resurrected bodies will be *supernatural* rather than *simply natural.* In this sense, our heavenly bodies will be imperishable, incorruptible, and immortal.

Furthermore, Paul is emphasizing that our resurrected

bodies will be dominated by the Holy Spirit, rather than dominated by hedonistic sensations or natural proclivities. In other words, our spiritual bodies will be bodies that are completely ruled by the Spirit, rather than enslaved to our sinful natures. In place of "sexual immorality, impurity and debauchery; idolatry and witchcraft; hatred, discord, jealousy, fits of rage, selfish ambition, dissensions, factions and envy; drunkenness, orgies, and the like" (Galatians 5:19–21), we will faithfully manifest the fruit of the Spirit, which is "love, joy, peace, patience, kindness, goodness, faithfulness, gentleness and self-control" (vv. 22–23).

Finally, having a resurrected spiritual body means being set free from our slavery to sin. Although Christians are declared positionally righteous before God, we continue to struggle against our sinful natures. Even the great apostle Paul, who wrote two-thirds of the New Testament epistles, confesses, "I have the desire to do what is good, but I cannot carry it out. For what I do is not the good I want to do; no, the evil I do not want to do—this I keep on doing" (Romans 7:18–19).

When we receive our spiritual bodies, what we are now only in position we will then be in practice. The prophet of Patmos put it this way: "There will be no more death or mourning or crying or pain, for the old order of things has passed away" (Revelation 21:4). The inspired prophet goes on to say that "nothing impure" will enter the new heaven and the new earth, "nor will anyone who does what is shameful or deceitful, but only those whose names are written in the Lamb's book of life" (v. 27).

In the meantime, we eagerly await the metamorphosis that will transform our natural bodies into bodies that are supernatural, Spirit dominated, and sin free.

SEVEN

"Resurrection" of the Cosmos

Then I saw a new heaven and a new earth, for the first heaven and the first earth had passed away, and there was no longer any sea. I saw the Holy City, the New Jerusalem, coming down out of heaven from God, prepared as a bride beautifully dressed for her husband. (Revelation 21:1–2)

ULTIMATELY, THE HOPE of the Christian is not only that God will resurrect our physical carcasses, but that he will also redeem the physical cosmos. In the words of Dr. John Piper, the hope of the historic Christian faith is "not the mere immortality of the soul, but rather the resurrection of the body and the renewal of all creation."[1] God's redemption is both the resurrection of the physical body and the renewal of this universe, including Planet Earth. The grand and glorious truth that we will once again walk this physical planet is made abundantly clear in Scripture. John's expression "a new heaven and a new earth" is not meant to communicate a place that is totally other than this present earth, but rather this universe renewed. Says

Anthony Hoekema: "Both in II Peter 3:13 and in Revelation 21:1 the Greek word used to designate the newness of the new cosmos is not *neos* but *kainos*. The word *neos* means new in time or origin, whereas the word *kainos* means new in nature or in quality. The expression *ouranon kainon kai gen kainen* ('a new heaven and a new earth,' Revelation 21:1) means, therefore, not the emergence of a cosmos totally other than the present one, but the creation of a universe which, though it has been gloriously renewed, stands in continuity with the present one."[2]

As there is continuity between our present bodies and our resurrected bodies, so too there will be continuity between the present physical universe and the one we will inhabit throughout eternity.

CONTINUITY

The principle of continuity begins with the resurrection of people and progresses through the renewal of this planet. Christ will not resurrect an entirely different group of human beings; rather, he will resurrect the very people who have populated this planet. In like manner, God will not renew another cosmos; rather, he will redeem the very world he once called "very good" (Genesis 1:31). John Piper points out that when Peter says that the present heavens and earth will pass away (see 2 Peter 3:10), he is communicating that the cosmos will be thoroughly transformed, as opposed to totally terminated:

> It does not have to mean that they go out of existence, but may mean that there will be such a change in them that their present condition passes away. We might say, "The caterpillar passes away, and the butterfly emerges." There is a real passing away, and there is a real continuity, a real connection.
>
> And when Peter says that this heaven and earth will be "destroyed" it does not have to mean entirely "put out of existence." We might say, "The flood destroyed many farms." But we don't mean that they vanished out of existence. We might say that on May 18, 1980, the immediate surroundings of Mt. St. Helens in Washington were destroyed by a blast 500 times more powerful than the Hiroshima atomic bomb. But anyone who goes there now and sees the new growth would know that "destroy" did not mean "put out of existence."
>
> And so what Peter may well mean is that at the

end of this age there will be cataclysmic events that bring this world to an end *as we know it*—not putting it out of existence, but wiping out all that is evil and cleansing it by fire and fitting it for an age of glory and righteousness and peace that will never end.[3]

Piper goes on to argue that this is precisely what Scripture has in mind. In Romans 8:22–23, Paul specifically connects the redemption of our physical bodies with the restoration of creation. Says Piper, "What happens to our bodies and what happens to the creation go together. And what happens to our bodies is not annihilation but redemption. . . . Our bodies will be redeemed, restored, made new, not thrown away. And so it is with the heavens and the earth."[4]

CONQUEST

Furthermore, we can rightly conclude that the cosmos will be renewed, not annihilated, on the basis of Christ's conquest over Satan on the cross. As Christ has liberated his children from death and disease, so too he will liberate his cosmos from destruction and decay. As Paul puts it in Romans 8, "the creation was subjected to frustration, not by its own choice, but by the will of the one who subjected it, in hope that the creation itself will be liberated from its bondage to decay" (vv. 20-21). This liberation, which begins with the conquest of the cross, will be completed at Christ's second coming. As Christ's conquest ensures our bodily resurrection, so too his conquest ensures the restoration of this cosmos:

> Indeed, in Scripture the resurrection of the body as a glorified body of flesh is inseparably tied to the renewal and glorification of the cosmos. In contrast to those who would declare this scriptural truth a myth, E. Thurneysen in 1931 expressed his faith in it when he wrote: "The world into which we shall enter in the Parousia of Jesus Christ is . . . not another world; it is this world, this heaven, this earth; both, however, passed away and renewed. It is these forests, these fields, these cities, these streets, these people, that will be the scene of redemption. At present they are battlefields, full of strife and sorrow of the not yet accomplished consummation; then they will be fields of victory, fields of harvest, where out of seed that was sown with tears the everlasting sheaves will be reaped and brought home."[5]

Anthony Hoekema further amplifies Christ's conquest by pointing out that if God annihilated the present cosmos, Satan would have won a decisive victory. He would have succeeded in so corrupting the cosmos that God would have had to completely do away with it. "But Satan did not win such a victory. On the contrary, Satan has been decisively defeated. God will reveal the full dimensions of that defeat when he shall renew this very earth on which Satan deceived mankind and finally banish from it all the results of Satan's evil machinations."[6]

CHILDBIRTH

A final assurance that God is not going to scrap this universe and start over with a brand-new one is communicated through the metaphor of childbirth. As Scripture puts it, "the whole creation has been groaning as in the pains of *childbirth* right up to the present time" (Romans 8:22; emphasis added). Paul uses the metaphor of childbirth to describe the longing of creation for the consummation of Christ's conquest on the cross. Says Piper, "Something is about to be brought forth *from* creation, not *in place* of creation. Creation is not going to be annihilated and recreated with no continuity. The earth is going to bring forth like a mother in labor (through the upheavals of fire and earthquake and volcanoes and pestilence and famine) a new earth."[7]

I don't know about you, but the more I think about the new heaven and the new earth, the more excited I get! It is incredible to think that one day soon we will not only experience the resurrection of our carcasses, but the renewal of the cosmos and the return of the Creator. We will literally have heaven on earth. Eden lost will become Eden restored and a whole lot more! Not only will we experience God's fellowship as Adam did, but we will see our Savior face to face. God incarnate will live in our midst. And we will never come to the end of exploring the infinite, inexhaustible I AM or the grandeur and glory of his incomparable creation.

Those who die in Christ will experience the new heaven and the new earth as both a physical place in creation and as the personal presence of the Creator: "The dwelling of God is with men, and he will live with them. They will be his people, and God himself will be with them and be their God. He will wipe every tear from their eyes. There will be no more death or mourning or crying or pain, for the old order of things has passed away. He who was seated on the throne said, 'I am making everything new!'" (Revelation 21:3–5).

Notes

INTRODUCTION

1.   Christ, the Creator of the cosmos, clearly communicated the horrifying reality that unbelievers will be physically resurrected to eternal conscious torment. "Do not be amazed," he said, "for a time is coming when all who are in their graves will hear his [Christ's] voice and come out—those who have done good will rise to live, and those who have done evil will rise to be condemned" (John 5:28–29; see also Matthew 25:41, 46; Luke 16:19–31; Revelation 14:11; 20:10). Hell is variously described as "darkness, where there will be weeping and gnashing of teeth" (Matthew 8:12); as a "fiery furnace" (Matthew 13:42); and as a "lake of burning sulfur" (Revelation 20:10). Its torment is said to be continuous (2 Thessalonians 1:9), unquenchable (Matthew 3:12), and eternal (Jude 7).

Therefore, Jesus said, "Repent and believe the good

news!" (Mark 1:15). For, "if you confess with your mouth, 'Jesus is Lord,' and believe in your heart that God raised him from the dead, you will be saved" (Romans 10:9).

Chapter 1. Mythologies

1. Hugh J. Schonfield, *The Passover Plot: A New Interpretation of the Life and Death of Jesus* (New York: Bernard Geis Associates, 1965).

2. Ibid., inside front cover flap.

3. Ibid., inside back cover flap.

4. Ibid., back cover.

5. Ibid.

6. Ibid., 13.

7. Lee Strobel, *The Case for Christ* (Grand Rapids: Zondervan, 1998), 192–93.

8. Gary R. Habermas, *The Historical Jesus: Ancient Evidence for the Life of Christ* (Joplin, Mo.: College Press Publishing Co., 1996), 73; J. P. Moreland, *Scaling the Secular City: A Defense of Christianity* (Grand Rapids: Baker Book House, 1987), 171.

9. D. H. Lawrence, *Love among the Haystacks and Other Stories* (New York: Penguin, 1960), 125, quoted in Strobel, *The Case for Christ,* 192.

10.   Donovan Joyce, *The Jesus Scroll* (New York: New American Library, 1972), quoted in Strobel, *The Case for Christ,* 192. In addition to citing the swoon hypotheses of D. H. Lawrence, Donovan Joyce, and Barbara Thiering, Strobel also cites Michael Baigent, Richard Leigh, and Henry Lincoln, *Holy Blood, Holy Grail* (New York: Delacorte, 1982), 372, in which Pontius Pilate was allegedly bribed to allow Jesus to be taken down from the cross before he died.

11.   Habermas, *The Historical Jesus,* 90–91.

12.   Barbara Thiering, *Jesus and the Riddle of the Dead Sea Scrolls: Unlocking the Secrets of His Life Story* (San Francisco: HarperSanFrancisco, 1992).

13.   Michael J. Wilkins and J. P. Moreland, eds., *Jesus Under Fire: Modern Scholarship Reinvents the Historical Jesus* (Grand Rapids: Zondervan, 1995), 210.

14.   The swoon and twin hypotheses are just two of many naturalistic accounts for the biblical data surrounding the resurrection of Christ. But all naturalistic accounts begin with a bias against the supernatural. Naturalistic accounts grow out of the antisupernatural environment fostered by the influential work of philosopher David Hume (1711–1776) in his famous arguments against miracles. An excellent presentation and

refutation of Hume's position can be found in R. Douglas Geivett and Gary R. Habermas, *In Defense of Miracles: A Comprehensive Case for God's Actions in History* (Downer's Grove, Ill.: InterVarsity Press, 1997).

15. Spelling for this name is uncertain—derived from William Lane Craig and Robert Greg Cavin, "Dead or Alive? A Debate on the Resurrection of Jesus" (Anaheim, Calif.: Simon Greenleaf University, 1995), audiotape.

16. Ibid.

17. Qur'an 4:157–59.

18. Norman L. Geisler and Abdul Saleeb, *Answering Islam: The Crescent in Light of the Cross* (Grand Rapids: Baker Book House, 1993), 65.

19. Ibid. *The Gospel of Barnabas* purports to be another first-century record of the life of Christ but is actually a late medieval invention with no bearing on the historical Jesus (see Geisler, *Answering Islam,* 295–99).

20. Ibid., 65–66 (see 64–67).

21. For an excellent presentation of the doctrines of the Jehovah's Witnesses and a refutation of them in light of historic biblical Christianity, see Walter Martin, *The Kingdom of the Cults,* Revised, Updated, Expanded Anniversary Edition

(Minneapolis: Bethany House Publishers, 1997), chap. 5.

22.   For a defense of the deity of Christ and the biblical doctrine of the Trinity against cultic constructs, see James R. White, *The Forgotten Trinity* (Minneapolis: Bethany House Publishers, 1998).

23.   *Let God Be True* (Brooklyn: Watchtower Bible and Tract Society, rev. ed. 1952), 138.

24.   Ibid., 41.

25.   *Things in Which It Is Impossible for God to Lie* (Brooklyn: Watchtower Bible and Tract Society, 1965), 354.

26.   Ibid., 355.

27.   *Studies in the Scriptures,* Series II (Allegheny, Penn.: Watchtower Bible and Tract Society, 1908), 129.

28.   *The Kingdom Is at Hand* (Brooklyn: Watchtower Bible and Tract Society, 1944), 259; cf. *Reasoning from the Scriptures* (Brooklyn: Watchtower Bible and Tract Society, 1985), 334.

29.   *From Paradise Lost to Paradise Regained* (Brooklyn: Watchtower Bible and Tract Society, 1958), 144.

30.   Josh McDowell, *The New Evidence That Demands a Verdict* (Nashville: Thomas Nelson Publishers, 1999), 203.

31.   Wilbur M. Smith, *Therefore Stand: Christian Apologetics* (Grand Rapids: Baker Book House, 1965), 369–70, quoted in

McDowell, *The New Evidence That Demands a Verdict,* 206–7.

32. Wilbur M. Smith, *Therefore Stand,* quoted in McDowell, *The New Evidence That Demands a Verdict,* 207.

33. Ibid.

CHAPTER 2. FATAL TORMENT

1. Habermas, *The Historical Jesus,* 143–70 (see esp. 158); Paul Copan, ed., *Will the Real Jesus Please Stand Up? A Debate between William Lane Craig and John Dominic Crossan* (Grand Rapids: Baker Book House, 1998), 26–27.

2. Except as noted, all following medical data and descriptions concerning Christ's suffering adapted from C. Truman Davis, "The Crucifixion of Jesus: The Passion of Christ from a Medical Point of View," *Arizona Medicine* (March 1965): 183–87; and William D. Edwards, Wesley J. Gabel, and Floyd E. Hosmer, "On the Physical Death of Jesus Christ," *The Journal of the American Medical Association* (21 March 1986): 1455–63.

3. Strobel, *The Case for Christ,* 197–98.

4. The spikes would have been driven either through Christ's palms, with wooden washers preventing his hands from tearing away, or through his wrists, which in Jewish understanding were part of the hands.

5. Strobel, *The Case for Christ,* 202.

6. Habermas, *The Historical Jesus,* 74. See Davis, "The Crucifixion of Jesus: The Passion of Christ from a Medical Point of View," 183–87; and Edwards, Gabel, and Hosmer, "On the Physical Death of Jesus Christ," 1455–63.

7. Habermas, *The Historical Jesus,* 72–73.

8. Ibid., 73.

9. Ibid., 73–74.

10. Ibid., 71.

Chapter 3. Empty Tomb

1. Wilkins and Moreland, *Jesus Under Fire*, 2.

2. Robert W. Funk, *Honest to Jesus* (San Francisco: HarperSanFrancisco, 1996), 305.

3. Interview by Mary Rourke, "Cross Examination," *Los Angeles Times,* 24 February 1994, E1, E5, quoted in Wilkins and Moreland, *Jesus Under Fire,* 2.

4. Richard N. Ostling, "Jesus Christ, Plain and Simple," *Time,* 10 January 1994, from the *Time* Web site at www.time.com (accessed 4 December 2002). See Wilkins and Moreland, *Jesus Under Fire,* 2.

5. "Facts About the Jesus Seminar and Founder Robert W.

Funk," Answers in Action Web site at www.answers.org/Apologetics / jesuseminar.html (accessed 17 December 1999).

6.   Ostling, "Jesus Christ, Plain and Simple"; Wilkins and Moreland, *Jesus Under Fire,* 142.

7.   Strobel, *The Case for Christ,* 114; Gregory A. Boyd, *Cynic Sage or Son of God?* (Wheaton: BridgePoint, 1995), 59–62.

8.   Boyd, *Cynic Sage or Son of God?* 62.

9.   Robert W. Funk, Roy W. Hoover, and the Jesus Seminar, *The Five Gospels* (New York: Macmillan Publishing Co., 1993), x.

10.   Gospel of Thomas, 114, in Funk, Hoover, and the Jesus Seminar, *The Five Gospels,* 532.

11.   James R. White, "The Jesus Seminar and the Gospel of Thomas: Courting the Media at the Cost of Truth," *Christian Research Journal* (Winter 1998): 51, available on Christian Research Institute's Web site at www.equip.org.

12.   See Gospel of Thomas, 114, cited above. As well, Dr. Gregory Boyd writes, "It is difficult to escape the conclusion that the talk about the 'the kingdom of God' or 'the kingdom of the Father' in GosThom [Gospel of Thomas] is often attributable to a gnostic-tending reworking of the canonical material. In GosThom, this phrase is taken to indicate 'the present secret religious knowledge of a heavenly world.' Hence, for example, the

Jesus of GosThom says, 'The Kingdom is inside of you, and it is outside of you. When you come to know yourselves, then you will become known, and you will realize that it is you who are the sons of the living Father. But if you will not know yourselves, you dwell in poverty and it is you who are that poverty' (GosThom, 3)" (Boyd, *Cynic Sage or Son of God?* 135).

13.   The Jesus Seminar is influenced by the view that the Gospel of Thomas (GosThom) does not depend on the canonical Gospels (Matthew, Mark, Luke, and John) and, in fact, predates Matthew and Luke in the first century. However, Dr. Gregory Boyd writes: "Numerous scholars . . . have argued that such a position is untenable. . . . In fact, most of the scholars who did the pioneering work on GosThom date it around A.D. 140. Among other considerations, we have no independent attestation of the existence of this work until the early third century when it is cited by Hippolytus and Origen—an unexpected silence if this is, in fact, a first-century work. What is more, GosThom reflects a distinct gnosticizing tendency which renders a second-century dating most feasible" (Boyd, *Cynic Sage or Son of God?* 134).

14.   Wilkins and Moreland, *Jesus Under Fire,* 142.

15.   John A. T. Robinson, *The Human Face of God*

(Philadelphia: Westminster, 1973), 131, quoted in Copan, *Will the Real Jesus Please Stand Up?* 27. And as scholar D. H. Van Daalen has noted, "It is extremely difficult to object to the empty tomb on historical grounds; those who deny it do so on the basis of theological or philosophical assumptions" (as quoted in William Lane Craig, "Contemporary Scholarship and the Historical Evidence for the Resurrection of Jesus Christ," *Truth* 1 (1985): 89–95, from the Leadership University Web site at http://www.leaderu.com/truth/1truth22. html; see D. H. Van Daalen, *The Real Resurrection* (London: Collins, 1970), 41, quoted in Wilkins and Moreland, *Jesus Under Fire,* 152).

16. Wilkins and Moreland, *Jesus Under Fire,* 148.

17. Ibid., 149.

18. Ibid., 148, 152.

19. Ibid., 147–48; See also Craig, "Contemporary Scholarship and the Historical Evidence." For arguments establishing early dates for the writing of Mark, see John Wehham, *Redating Matthew, Mark & Luke* (Downers Grove: Ill.: InterVarsity Press, 1992), chaps. 6–8; Boyd, *Cynic Sage or Son of God?* chap. 11.

20. Wilkins and Moreland, *Jesus Under Fire,* 147. In an interview with investigative journalist Lee Strobel, Craig

notes that the confession used by Paul is incredibly early and therefore trustworthy. Craig goes on to point out that "essentially, it's a four-line formula. The first line refers to the Crucifixion, the second to the burial, the third to the Resurrection, and the fourth to Jesus' appearances. . . . This creed is actually a summary that corresponds line for line with what the gospels teach. When we turn to the gospels, we find multiple, independent attestation of this burial story, and Joseph of Arimathea is specifically named in all four accounts. On top of that, the burial story in Mark is so extremely early that it's simply not possible for it to have been subject to legendary corruption" (Strobel, *The Case for Christ,* 209). See pp. 42–46 for a discussion of the pre-Pauline creed in 1 Corinthians 15:3–7; see Habermas, *The Historical Jesus,* chap. 7.

21. Strobel, *The Case for Christ,* 217.

22. Ibid., 218.

23. William Lane Craig, *Reasonable Faith* (Wheaton: Crossway Books, 1994), 276.

24. Ibid.

25. Ronald F. Youngblood, gen. ed., *Nelson's New Illustrated Bible Dictionary* (Nashville: Thomas Nelson Publishers, 1995),

1318. It is in part because of first-century Jewish attitudes toward women that liberal scholars dated the Gospels so late, even into the second century, believing that the Gospel accounts of the women's testimony must have been made up. Indeed, if the women's testimony had not been so overwhelmingly persuasive, it would have been dismissed.

26.   Craig S. Keener, *The IVP Bible Background Commentary: New Testament* (Downers Grove, Ill.: InterVarsity Press, 1993), 210.

27.   Youngblood, *Nelson's New Illustrated Bible Dictionary,* 1318.

28.   Paragraph adapted from Wilkins and Moreland, *Jesus Under Fire,* 152.

29.   Paragraph adapted from Habermas, *The Historical Jesus,* 205–6.

30.   Paragraph adapted from Wilkins and Moreland, *Jesus Under Fire,* 146–47.

CHAPTER 4. APPEARANCES OF CHRIST

1.   Wilkins and Moreland, *Jesus Under Fire*, 147.

2.   Habermas, *The Historical Jesus,* 154; cf. Wilkins and Moreland, *Jesus Under Fire,* 42–43, 147.

3. Habermas, *The Historical Jesus,* 153–54.

4. Gary R. Habermas and Antony G. N. Flew, *Did Jesus Rise from the Dead?* (San Francisco: Harper and Row, 1987), 86.

5. Strobel, *The Case for Christ,* 230. See Joachim Jeremias, "Easter: The Earliest Tradition and the Earliest Interpretation," *New Testament Theology: The Proclamation of Jesus,* trans. by John Bowden (New York: Scribner's, 1971), 306; Ulrich Wilckens, *Resurrection* (Atlanta: John Knox Press, 1978), 2.

6. Craig, *Reasonable Faith,* 285; see A. N. Sherwin-White, *Roman Society and Roman Law in the New Testament* (Oxford: Clarendon, 1963), 188–91.

7. Adapted from Craig, *Reasonable Faith,* 285.

8. Herodotus (c. 484–424 B.C.) was an important Greek historian.

9. Craig, *Reasonable Faith,* 285.

10. Julius Müller, *The Theory of Myths, in Its Application to the Gospel History Examined and Confuted* (London: John Chapman, 1844), 26, quoted in Craig, *Reasonable Faith,* 285.

11. Craig, *Reasonable Faith,* 285 (emphasis added).

12. Strobel, *The Case for Christ,* 233.

13. See 1 Corinthians 15:3–7. Paul received this creed from the believing community (v. 3), perhaps from Peter and

James in Jerusalem (see Galatians 1:18–19), if not sooner (see Habermas, *The Historical Jesus,* 155).

14. C. H. Dodd, "The Appearances of the Risen Christ: A Study in the Form Criticism of the Gospels," *More New Testament Studies* (Manchester: University of Manchester, 1968), 128; quoted in Craig, *Reasonable Faith,* 282.

15. Craig, *Reasonable Faith,* 282.

16. Youngblood, *Nelson's New Illustrated Bible Dictionary,* 955.

17. Discussion adapted from Craig, *Reasonable Faith,* 281–83.

18. Ibid., 281–82 (emphasis in original).

19. Ibid., 283. See Josephus, *Antiquities of the Jews,* 20:200, quoted in Craig, *Reasonable Faith,* 283.

20. Adapted from Craig, *Reasonable Faith,* 283.

21. Hans Grass, *Ostergeschehen und Osterberichte,* 4th ed. (Gottingen: Vandenhoeck & Ruprecht, 1974), 80, quoted in Craig, *Reasonable Faith,* 283.

22. Michael Martin, *The Case Against Christianity* (Philadelphia: Temple University Press, 1991), 94.

23. Ibid., 94–95.

24. Rick Joyner, "The Heart of David: Worship and Warfare," Conference Report (April 1996), audiotape.

25. Ibid.

26. Ibid.

27. Habermas and Flew, *Did Jesus Rise from the Dead?* 50. (Habermas cites personal correspondence from Dr. Collins, 21 February 1977.)

28. Ibid., 51. Habermas also cites J. P. Brady, "The Veridicality of Hypnotic, Visual Hallucinations," in Wolfram Keup, *Origin and Mechanisms of Hallucinations* (New York: Plenum Press, 1970), 181; Weston La Barre, "Anthropological Perspectives on Hallucination and Hallucinogens," quoted in *Hallucinations: Behavior, Experience and Theory,* ed. R. K. Siegel and L. J. West (New York: John Wiley and Sons, 1975), 9–10.

29. Strobel, *The Case for Christ,* 239.

30. Craig, *Reasonable Faith,* 292.

31. Ibid., 292–93. In Jewish thought, the resurrection was only general, after the end of the world, and void of any conception of an isolated resurrection for Messiah (Ibid., 290–91).

32. E.g., Atheist Morton Smith wrote an entire book trying to show that Jesus employed hypnosis and other sociopsychological manipulation tactics to dupe his devotees (see Morton Smith, *Jesus the Magician* [San Francisco: Harper and Row, 1978]).

33. Charles T. Tart, "Transpersonal Potentialities of Deep Hypnosis," *Journal of Transpersonal Psychology,* no. 1 (1970): 37.

34. Discussion adapted from Hank Hanegraaff, *Counterfeit Revival: Looking for God in all the Wrong Places* (Dallas: W Publishing Group, 1997), pt. 5, 221, 239.

35. Robert W. Marks, *The Story of Hypnotism* (Grand Rapids: Prentice-Hall, 1947), 190.

36. Ibid., 191.

37. Ibid., 193.

38. Ibid., 195.

39. Charles Baudouin, *Suggestion and Autosuggestion* (London: George Allen and Unwin, 1954), 82.

40. Discussion adapted from Hanegraaff, *Counterfeit Revival,* 235–36.

41. Marks, *The Story of Hypnotism,* 150.

42. Ibid.

43. Baghwan Shree Rajneesh, *Fear Is the Master,* Jeremiah Films, 1986, video.

44. Carl Braaten, *History and Hermeneutics,* vol. 2 of *New Directions in Theology Today,* ed. William Hordern (Philadelphia: Westminster Press, 1966), 78, quoted in Habermas and Flew, *Did Jesus Rise from the Dead?* 24.

45. Elizabeth L. Hillstrom, *Testing the Spirits* (Downers Grove, Ill.: InterVarsity Press, 1995), 79.

46. Gradations of hypnotizability range from zero (almost no hypnotizability) to five (extremely hypnotizable). See Jon Trott, "The Grade Five Syndrome," *Cornerstone,* vol. 20, no. 96. Discussion adapted from Hanegraaff, *Counterfeit Revival,* 237–38.

47. This information was summarized from a variety of sources, including Dr. George Ganaway, "Historical Versus Narrative Truth," *Journal of Dissociation* II, no. 4 (December 1989): 205–20, and Steven Jay Lynn and Judith W. Rhue, "Fantasy Proneness," *American Psychologist* (January 1988): 35–44.

48. Judith W. Rhue and Steven Jay Lynn, "Fantasy Proneness, Hypnotizability, and Multiple Personality" in *Human Suggestibility,* ed. John F. Schumaker (New York: Routledge, 1991), 201.

49. Trott, "The Grade Five Syndrome," 16.

50. Habermas and Flew, *Did Jesus Rise from the Dead?* 22.

51. Norman Perrin, *The Resurrection according to Matthew, Mark, and Luke* (Philadelphia: Fortress, 1977), 80, quoted in Paul Copan, *Will the Real Jesus Please Stand Up?* 28 (emphasis added).

CHAPTER 5. TRANSFORMATION

1. Source unknown.

2. Simon Greenleaf, *The Testimony of the Evangelists: The Gospels Examined by the Rules of Evidence* (Grand Rapids: Kregel Classics, 1995; originally published 1874), 31–32.

3. See 1 Corinthians 15:5, in which the original apostles, minus Judas, are referred to as the Twelve (cf. John 20:24).

4. See Clement of Rome (c. A.D. 30–100), *First Epistle to the Corinthians,* chap. V; Tertullian (c. 160–225), *On Prescription Against Heretics,* chap. xxxvi; Eusebius (c. 260–340), *History of the Church,* Bk. II: XXV.

5. See Eusebius, *History of the Church,* Bk. III: I, where Eusebius quotes Origen (c. 185–254) concerning Peter's crucifixion.

6. Kenneth Barker, gen. ed., *The NIV Study Bible* (Grand Rapids: Zondervan, 1985), 1879.

7. Eusebius, Bk. II: XXIII. Cf. Josephus, *Antiquities,* 20:9:1; see John P. Meier, *A Marginal Jew: Rethinking the Historical Jesus*, vol. 1 (New York: Doubleday, 1991), 57–59.

8. Strobel, *The Case for Christ,* 251.

9. Norman Geisler and Thomas Howe, *When Critics Ask*

(Wheaton: Victor Books, 1992), 78. See Matthew 28:1–10; John 20:19, 26; Acts 2:1; 20:7; 1 Corinthians 16:2.

10.   Discussion adapted from Strobel, *The Case for Christ,* 251, 253.

11.   Carl F. H. Henry, ed., *Basic Christian Doctrines* (Grand Rapids: Baker Book House, 1971), 256.

12.   See also Matthew 28:19; Acts 8:16; 10:48; 19:5; Romans 6:3–5; 1 Corinthians 6:11.

13.   Adapted from Strobel, *The Case for Christ,* 253.

Chapter 6. Resurrection of Believers

1.   Adapted from Peter Kreeft, *Everything You Ever Wanted to Know about Heaven . . . But Never Dreamed of Asking* (San Francisco: Ignatius Press, 1990), 84–85.

2   Norman L. Geisler, *The Battle for the Resurrection* (Nashville: Thomas Nelson Publishers, 1992), 63.

3.   Ibid., emphasis in original.

4.   Joni Eareckson Tada, *Heaven . . . Your Real Home* (Grand Rapids: Zondervan, 1995), 36–37.

5.   DNA provides one possible means for explaining the blueprint for the resurrection body.

6.   Scripture makes it clear that graves will be emptied (see

Matthew 28:6; John 5:28–29; cf. Matthew 27:52–53). It is possible that God will use new particles, in part, in resurrecting our bodies, but most assuredly he will utilize those particles from our current bodies that are *available* (e.g., bones). Cf. Ezekiel 37:1–14.

7. Norman L. Geisler, *Baker Encyclopedia of Christian Apologetics* (Grand Rapids: Baker Book House, 1999), 658.

8. Ibid. Augustine writes of the spiritual body: "They will be spiritual, not because they shall cease to be bodies, but because they shall subsist by the quickening spirit" (*The City of God,* XIII:22, in Philip Schaff, ed., *Nicene and Post-Nicene Fathers,* First Series, vol. II [Grand Rapids: Wm. B. Eerdmans Publishing Co., reprinted 1983], 257). When Paul says, "flesh and blood cannot inherit the kingdom of God" (1 Corinthians 15:50), he is not denying the physical nature of the resurrection. Rather, he is using a common Jewish metaphor to express mortality. "Flesh and blood" is "perishable," while the "kingdom of God" is "imperishable." His point is that it would be impossible for mortal humans to inherit the new heaven and new earth without a metamorphosis. (See Edmond Charles Gruss, *Apostles of Denial* [Grand Rapids: Baker Book House, 1978 reprint], 136–37.)

9. Kreeft, *EverythingYou EverWanted to Know about Heaven,* 90.

10. Ibid., 91.

11. Hoekema, *The Bible and the Future* (Grand Rapids: Wm. B. Eerdmans Publishing Co., 1979), 250.

CHAPTER 7.
"RESURRECTION" OF THE COSMOS

1. John Piper, *Future Grace* (Sisters, Ore.: Multnomah Publishers, 1995), 374.

2 Hoekema, *The Bible and the Future,* 280.

3. Piper, *Future Grace,* 376.

4. Ibid., 378.

5. J. A. Schep, *The Nature of the Resurrection Body* (Grand Rapids: Wm. B. Eerdmans Publishing Co., 1964), 218–19. Schep writes, "It is on *this* earth, transformed by God's almighty power into a suitable dwelling place for believers in their glorified bodies, that 'God himself shall be with them, and be their God . . .' (Revelation 21:3ff.). It is *this* earth that the meek will inherit, according to the promise of Jesus (Matthew 5:5)." (Ibid., 218, emphasis in original.)

6. Hoekema, *The Bible and the Future,* 281.

7. Piper, *Future Grace,* 377–78 (emphasis in original).